Faye Kitariev, M.D.

CHOREOGRAPHY
of
AWAKENING

Foreword by Steve Chandler
The best-selling author of *Time Warrior*.

Enchanted Garden Press
Irvine, California, 2014

Enchanted Garden Press
Irvine, CA 92612

Printed in the United States of America
Original cover illustration by Dmitri Kitariev

The events and experiences detailed herein have either been
rendered as the author has remembered them or are the
product of the author's imagination. Some names, identities
and circumstances have been changed in order to protect the
privacy and/or anonymity of the various individuals involved.

Praise for *Choreography of Awakening*

"This beautifully written book is filled with simple wisdom I am certain will enrich your life. It is a testimonial that any path traveled with openness rather than resistance to life's experience is a worthy road to travel. And I love the way Faye weaved her figure skating metaphors into the fabric."

~**H. Ronald Hulnick, Ph.D.,** President, University of Santa Monica and Co-Author of *Loyalty To Your Soul*

"I highly recommend this passionate book...sit back and allow Faye Kitariev's poetic energy as a storyteller to choreograph your own dance of transformation and excitement for a future full of possibilities."

~**Steve Chandler**, the author of *Time Warrior*

"Faye Kitariev is a brilliant artist and coach and helped me achieve so many of my dreams and overcome multiple struggles. Her strength and brilliance are an inspiration on and off the ice. This book can help anyone believe in themself and believe in their power within."

~**Johnny Weir**, 3 times US National Figure Skating Champion, 2-Time Olympic Competitor, World Bronze Medalist, Movie and TV Star

"Faye Kitariev's book is an inspirational journey of artistry and sport! A must read for anyone looking to inspire themselves to a greater understanding!"

~**Phillip Mills**, World & Olympic Figure Skating Choreographer

After reading this book, not only do I feel validated in my own feelings of spirituality and community with the Divine through movement and choreography within my own skating, but I feel inspired to continue on the path of growth and learning in all aspects of my life... Inspired to seek out change and knowledge; embrace the possibilities that can become realities when I reflect on past experiences, own my fears, and find the "why's" behind my future "wants".

I believe the principals explained within *"Choreography of Awakening"* are both enlightening and illuminating, stirring the soul, spirit and mind.

A must read!

~**Wesley Campbell**, 11 time U.S. National Figure Skating Competitor

"Faye's book makes you realize that it is possible to attain your life goals no matter what the situation, she has a deep passion for everything she does, and I was truly inspired."

~**Galit Chait-Moracci**, World Bronze Figure Skating Medalist, 3-time Olympic Competitor, World and Olympic Coach

"Faye has a gift for seeing the impossible as possible, and for creating a picture of that possibility for all of us to experience. It is easy to see how she so successfully coached young skaters to the levels of excellence they achieved. Using story, metaphor, intuition and humor, she shows us her own courageous journey, both on the external from immigrant to coach of stars, but more importantly on the inner journey, the life long journey, to authentic success. Once I started it, I couldn't put it down."

~**Rory Cohen, MPH, MA, SCPC**, President, take-10now.com, the author of *Take 10: How to Achieve Your Someday Dreams in 10 Minutes a Day*

"Coach Faye Kitariev in the most humble way, shares her personal journey as a young Russian skater, to a championship coach, giving us an inside look at the world of Championship figure skating, and her own process of self-discovery. "Choreography of Awakening" inspires us with its unmistakable message, discovered along the way by the author, that "There are no limits to human potential". This book can change your life."

~**Christopher Connolly, MA**, University of Santa Monica Faculty Member, Writer & Composer

"Faye Kitariev presents us a wonderful example of what it takes for one to process their life experience. She bravely moves into the biggest of life's questions; "What has my life experience given me? Who am I choosing to become? What does my future hold in relation to my life purpose?" These are not easy questions, but Faye knows that the key to life, is to go through a process that makes sense of it all. I am touched by her authenticity and courage. Her writing flows smoothly and the skating metaphor can be applied to all of our lives. I know that I am not alone in expressing gratitude that this Dragon has awakened!"

~**Mark "Dr. DREAM" Peebler**, International Speaker, Radio Host, Holistic Healing Practitioner

"Every so often, a book comes along that can't help but improve your life. Faye Kitariev's *A Choreography of Awakening* is one such book. Faye interweaves words of wisdom with hard-earned personal experience to lead readers on an enlightening journey of discovery. With each heartfelt chapter, readers will feel a transformation, and if they don't, Faye's insightful practice lessons at the end of every chapter are sure to help them along. Take the time to read this rare gem. You'll be glad you did."

~**Ken Dickson**, the Author of *"Detour from Normal"*

Contents

For Abbie
Who is my endless source of love and inspiration every day
For my Mom and Dad
Who would be proud

Dear Kathleen,
With all my love –
Blessings of courage, strength of heart, joy and wisdom!
There is genius in you! Let it awaken! Life happens outside the comfort zone! Listen to your heart!

Love & Light
Faye

If life was a choreographed dance between the doing and the being.

If you could choreograph your own 'dance'.

If you could perform it at your highest potential

What would it look like?...

Foreword

The joy of self expression

There is a reason we follow athletes so avidly. There is a reason the Olympics are so enthusiastically watched. The joyful fullness of self-expression is something our own soul longs for. We see it on the playing field...and on the ice.

Even though I am a typical clumsy unsophisticated American male, watching football and playing basketball when I can, I am always drawn to the Olympic skaters—like the ones coached by Faye Kitariev, like the ones so dramatically described in this book, the *Choreography of Awakening*.

There is always a fierce but gentle physical poetry in the skating competitions, such exciting displays of grace and collapse, surges of glory and the sinking downward spiral of tragic failure, all in one inspired musical whirl on ice!

The metaphor here for awakening the human spirit is irresistible. This is life itself, at its most beautiful, tragic and heroic...all set to music!

Coach Faye's story is compelling because it is a story of awakening. Her career as a successful sports coach was deepened and enhanced by another journey she was taking..the journey of the soul to enlightenment.

Her early gravitation to the study of the Tao harmonized perfectly with the "angels" she was coaching to success in competition. In this she was not unlike the great American basketball coach Phil Jackson who brought his own Zen enlightenment into his championship-level coaching of Michael Jordan of the Bulls and Shaquille O'Neal and Kobe Bryant of the Los Angeles Lakers.

And the spiritual depth is not inconsequential. Even though many other coaches consider such depth a kind of new age eccentric affectation, it's hard to ignore the results.

When one begins the kind of path Coach Faye began, metaphors for the highest possible life begin to appear everywhere. Everything in life becomes a Tony Robbins fire-walking seminar—producing insights and breakthroughs and joy upon joy.

Faye's story of the skater Galit is so powerful. What it taught Faye it also teaches the reader.

"Some people would quietly laugh at Galit behind her back, judging her as naive and weird. After all she had no talent, lacked flow and flexibility, and frankly wasn't going anywhere, no matter how hard she tried."

But she kept trying. Even though she finished a distant 28th in her first World Championship. When she kept on the path of purposeful practice, holding to a devoted dream, Faye watched with interest. Then she watched with envy. Finally, she watched Galit with a sense of wonder. Why? Why stay on the path?

The one night in 2002, Galit did it. She won a medal in the World Championship and Faye leaped and screamed for joy. The message from the universe was unmistakeable. The metaphor sang out to Faye: "There are no limits in human potential, there are limits in human beliefs!"

The stories of skaters in this book all hold fascinating lessons in psychological pain and triumph. As she coaches her skaters in the art and sport of life itself, we, as readers feel the journey, the falls, and the uplifting successes.

Faye does not spare herself, here, either. She is vulnerable and forthcoming. Her innocence is a perfect match for her power as a coach and mentor and spirit guide...not just to the athlete, but the human being inside the athlete.

The author must have foreseen the sense of inspiration that gets produced by the end of each chapter, because it offers short thought experiments that allow us to go deeper into the insight each chapter inspires. These exercises are usually the part I skip in "self-help" books, but here they are too compelling to ignore. Readers who follow these guided mind exercises (soul exercises, heart exercises) will enjoy them, to say the least.

If this were merely a sports book, people would read it and enjoy it on that level. After all, who would not want to hear the inside story of what it was like to train and coach such a charismatic international champion as Sasha Cohen?

But this book is more than that. It is a spiritual biography. It is a travel diary...the journey of a soul whose only quest all along was to learn.

The great novelist Vladimir Nabokov once described a spiral as "a liberated circle." I don't know why that quotation came to mind as I read this book a second time. Maybe the image is just perfect for the spiraling beauty of Faye Kitariev's sport, especially for the athletes she has touched with her beginner's mind.

It is extremely good news that Faye Kitariev has expanded her professional reach into the world of "soul-centered" professional life coaching. Now it will be all of us who have a chance to work with her and liberate the vicious circles our worried minds keep us in. As you'll see when you read this book, her guidance is a gift.

Steve Chandler
Phoenix, Arizona
2013

Introduction

It was in early fall of 2005. I was teaching dedicated, committed-to-excellence, driven-to-success little soldiers, their hair pinned in tight buns, clothed in beautiful little dresses, skating in a freezing ice rink in Southern California during ungodly morning hours. We were going through the usual morning drills designed to prepare them for their biggest event of the year: Southwest Pacific Regionals. I was hoping to have three of my girls qualify for the prestigious Junior Nationals. The rumor spread that day that a renowned skater - Sasha Cohen, had returned home to Southern California. She reunited again with her long-time coach, world-famous John Nicks, after venturing out to the East Coast to skate under the tutelage of Russian trainer Tatiana Tarasova.

I loved Sasha and was inspired by her unmatched artistry. She was a very determined athlete, although she had some difficulty staying calm under pressure. But forgive me, I am going off-track with my story, just like then, during the dark, cold morning freestyle session in Yorba Linda. "Is it really that important for me to know about Sasha right now, when all of my mental energy needs to be directed towards preparation for Regionals?" I felt a slight rush of irritation. Then, boom! I got called off the ice by the rink manager.

"Mr. Nicks is on the line. He wants to talk to you." Mr. Nicks, not only world-renowned figure skating coach, but also the director of skating in two facilities, one of which is in Yorba Linda where I was teaching. I walked towards the box office to answer the call. My knees were weak, and my heart beat fast. I anticipated the worst and had the full support of my inner critic: "What did I do wrong this time? Am I in trouble? Of course, you are! One doesn't usually get called upon by the director of skating, especially one of Mr. Nicks' stature, unless you are in serious trouble!" I felt my heart skip a beat. I took the receiver, and a deep breath.

"Yes, Mr. Nicks. This is Faye."

"Good morning, Faye." His voice was calm and poised, cracking with a Brit's accent he couldn't lose after many years living in America. "I'd like to ask you for a favor." Pause. Eternity passed. My brain tried to grasp the meaning of what that could mean, what favor he could possibly ask of me, a nobody! "Could you come down here to work with Sasha on some choreography?" OMG! Me? With Sasha?! My heart started racing like a shy 15-year-old invited to the prom by her secret crush! Part of me wanted to sabotage the opportunity right there on the spot; the other part agreed. "You are an amazing choreographer. You know it! Go for it!"

"Sure, Mr. Nicks, I would love that! When would be the best time for me to come over?"

I was a young, driven, ambitious, up-and-coming, talented coach. My goals were clear. Every day I went to work with a mission. Every moment I was awake I thought of ways to improve my game. In every student I taught I saw a potential Olympic champion. But I saw it all in the sequence of taking a small child, teaching and guiding them through the levels of figure skating competition in order: No-test, Pre-Preliminary, Preliminary......Junior, Senior.....Many years of pain and growth. It never occurred to me that there was a possibility that a high-profile athlete would just "knock on my door," so to speak, and ask me, "Could you meet me in Italy tomorrow?" A scenario like this only happens in fairy tales where a poor peasant girl becomes a princess, where their lives transform, and they flourish forever in the "happily-ever-after". My mother systematically told me, "You are on your own. Depend solely on yourself." I had adopted my mother's rule without question and learned to work hard and be dependent exclusively upon myself. I didn't believe in miracles and certainly was not going to rely on any in order to move closer to my dream.

Well, my mother was......wrong! Miracles do happen, and I was fortunate enough to experience that! I thought, "Wow, is it really happening? Is my dream really coming true?"

Little did I know then that this early morning call from Mr. Nicks and a resulting trip to Italy with Sasha would begin a completely new chapter in my life and would give me the meaning and a purpose I couldn't even begin to imagine. But all about that later.....

This book is about the journey, a journey to success and self-growth, a journey of making the impossible possible, a journey of realizing dreams along the way.

This book is also a journey in itself, as my life started unfolding in an unpredictable way at the same time I was writing it. It began with the intention of being an inspirational guide in personal development for figure skaters, their coaches, and parents. But just as my life's path wasn't straight, the path this book took turned out to resemble the yellow brick road of Oz. From the beginning I decided to allow the Great Spirit to guide me and I would surrender to its order and flow in the direction it decided to take me in. It was in the Spirit's resolve to use my story as a figure skating coach to become a messenger and a guide to people who, like me, are seeking their meaning and purpose in life. You will find here many stories and messages unfolding as I taught live lessons to the skaters on the ice, or to non-skaters off the ice. If you are a skater, see how you can adopt some of the principals to your own skating. If you are on the path of other achievements, just substitute "skating" for whatever you do and use "skating" as a parable. Sometimes I write about a specific skating element. Don't let that scare you if you don't know what it means. Every jump I describe is just an experience, a tool, so to speak, that is really used to assist the practitioner to move towards growth and expansion in their own field of life. Don't worry:

"It will all work out in the end, and if it hasn't worked out, it's not the end," as Kezziah Lloret said.

I have a knack for choreography, a seventh sense, so to speak, and this book has been my biggest "choreography" project yet, my "Senior Long Program"! Just like creating a new program, you show up with the music and a theme but have no idea how it will unfold. There are basic guidelines on how many elements should be in the program, the type of elements, and its difficulty. Then the process of creation begins, and I have always intuited the spirit of the music, spirit of an athlete, and my own spirit, to be the guide. I surrendered to this energy that is beyond me for guidance and arrived at a very profound, meaningful composition. It has never failed, and intuitively I used a similar approach to the writing of this book.

Choreography of Awakening is about getting out of your own way to move towards where you are 'supposed' to go. It is a "Choreographed Program" that covers some of the basic elements required by the sport called LIFE. The elements vary in the degree of difficulty and are set within the context of the program. They are the chapters in this book. Then there are footwork and transitions, which really are the meat of the program. They are what make the program interesting and flowing. In skating language it is called Program Components. These include Skating Skills, Transitions, Choreography, Interpretation, and Performance. The components are what connect an audience to the skater. In this book that would be the stories within each chapter. It was my intention to create the setting where you could not only learn the concepts but actually experience each story on a deeper level. Every one of them carries an insight open to your 'Interpretation,' or contemplation. To assist you in anchoring your realizations, you are invited to work your process through a series of questions or exercises presented at the end of each chapter - practices.

The degree of excellence that you will achieve or have already achieved in each of the elements or Program Components, will determine your personal success in this lifetime. I am not talking about the kind of success where the number of dollars earned, medals received, cars driven, houses lived in, or even positions held determine whether or not you were successful. I am talking about the kind of success where you can look at your life and say, "I am fulfilled! I am happy! My life was meaningful and complete!"

Don't be fooled by the biographical nature of some stories. Each was written with the intention of delivering a message. Read open-mindedly and ask yourself, "Is there a message for me? Why do I need to know this now?"

I named the chapters after the elements of skating, such as double Axel and triple Salchow. The content of the chapter doesn't really have anything to do with the particular jump or spin, although I do give a brief introduction to what the element is in the *TABLE OF CONTENTS DECODED* at the end of the book. Each chapter is about a specific theme, such as Purpose, Inspiration, Vision, Decisions, Fear, Beliefs, etc. By choosing the names for my chapters, I intend to challenge you to use your imagination to make an association between the name of the element and the story. Such is the intention of the choreographer: to create a story to the music, and then let the audience interpret what it was all about. Oftentimes the choreographer tells one story; the skater skates his own; and the audience understands it yet in another way. The way that you will understand is exactly the way it should be understood by you. Let yourself absorb the energy; connect with it. Let your heart guide you. Become aware and present to how you feel inside your body. What emotions are you experiencing? Why? What moves you? What inspires you? What makes you frown?

I am now ready to invite you to skate this Long Program with me. Perhaps some of you have already skated this program. That's okay. When I coach my athletes, they have to practice their programs over and over again to attain some degree of mastery and confidence. And no matter how many times they have skated their programs, they never fail to learn something new in the process. Some parts of the program become their favorites, and others less so, but it is only through the relentless practice, love, and commitment, a master will emerge. I hope that, with this book, I can help you to uncover your hidden potential, help you to become aware of the fire within you, ready to break out and conquer the world. It is my goal to inspire you to go find out what you are made of and why you are here.

Remember, not everyone has the potential to be better than everybody else, but everyone has the potential to be the best he/she can be. That measure of success is available to every person! I invite you now to "put your skates on" - to open your heart and your mind to the unlimited possibilities hidden within you, and step through the doorway onto the beautiful clean white ice to skate your Long Program.

Prologue

It is a warm, sunny morning in the dry sand desert some-where in Arizona. Our group is walking behind the guide through the sand dunes to the point of our destination. "How does he know where to go?" I wonder, looking around me at the homogeneous landscape. Orange sand is in front, behind, and on both sides of me, stretching as far as I can see, only contrasting with the startling blue of the sky. Never before have I seen such a beautiful contrast of colors in natural life as the contrast here. The desert pallete almost doesn't look real. The orange makes the blue so clear, bright, and sharp, just like I've seen on the paintings at the street fair. I judged those artists as amateurs, as if they exaggerated colors, but now I am sorry I judged them. Here these colors are very real.

Our guide leads confidently forward, without slowing down even for a moment to see if we are still behind him. I speed up my pace. My short legs have difficulty competing with his long 6'5" giant stride. He did not announce what adventure was awaiting us in the desert but did let us know that it will be a worthwhile trip. In the past, when we took journeys with him, we were not disappointed. This time, he promised, when we leave the desert later this evening, we will be forever transformed. I have no idea what he was talking about, but it felt good and my heart skipped a beat in a wave of excitement. A few more minutes on this walk and he announces our destination. Okay so this is it. We walked for over half an hour to the place that looked exactly as any other place around here, all special in exactly the same way. We stop and put our backpacks and blankets down, and sit down. Our guide gives a talk regarding the sacredness of this land to the community of local Indian tribes who have lived in this territory for thousands of years. He asks us to look around and points to a couple of landmarks: a snowy hilltop glistening in the north and a long red mesa in the south. "Now," he says, looking at us intently, "it's time for you to go on your journey. It is 10:00 in the morning. You will go into the desert by yourself, wherever your heart leads you, and we will try to get back together here before 4:00 p.m. I will beat the drum, and you will hear me from miles away. Follow the sound of the drum to come back."

Okay, go where? Orange sand, everywhere the same. My husband Dima starts to walk towards the mesa. I follow him. I find myself being afraid to get lost all by myself in the desert. After about 10 minutes I stop. I hear my inner voice speak:

"You are not a follower. You are a leader. You have your own head. Find your special way."

"Fine," I say, "then lead me, if you insist. Where do you want me to go?"

"Listen to the wind. It will show you."

The wind? That is an interesting idea. I imagine myself being a character from some adventure book.

"Wind, wind, show me the way," I say half jokingly.

To my surprise, the perfectly still air starts moving, talking.

"Shhhhhhhhhh," it whispers, and all of a sudden I notice that the desert is not just orange sand, but there are little plants and bushes that move in response to the wind, as if showing me where to go next. I follow. I don't pay attention to where it is taking me. It doesn't really matter. I am going to wander around this desert all in my pristine solitude with my thoughts for six hours. Six hours seems like a long time, six hours and no one to talk to. I walk, following, "Shhhhhhhh," to the right and to the left, north and south. Then the wind commands me to stop. I stop. The air is filled with peaceful stillness. Nothing is moving. "Did you want me to stop right here?" I yell out into the nothingness.

"Shhh." ("Yes," I translate).

"What do I need to do here?"

"Shhh," the wind responds. I translate it, "Sit down." I sit.

"Now what? I am sitting."

"Shhhhh." ("Look around you.")

I look around. Not far from me I see a good-sized bush. My gaze stops at this bush. The wind gives me an encouragement. This was the reason to stop in this spot. I look at the bush closely, and now I see a sleeping dragon, resting peacefully among the dunes.

"I see a sleeping dragon," I yell to the wind. "Is this it?"

"Shhh," ("Yes," whistles the wind.)

"What do I need to know about this dragon?"

"Shhhhhh." ("You are a sleeping dragon.")

"I am a sleeping dragon?" I say in disbelief.

"Shhh." ("Yes.")

"What do I need to do with it?"

"Shhhhh." ("Wake it up!")

I am overwhelmed. There is a sleeping dragon inside of me, and I have to wake it up. It's not just a dragon; it is sleeping. It is snoozing comfortably in its dwelling, but it will have to wake up. Then what? They like flying, don't they? Dragons fly! They breathe fire, fire breath. I practice breath of fire in yoga, to awaken a special energy within me. Is this why I am drawn to this practice? Did I always know that there is sleeping dragon within me?

"Shhhhhhhhhhhhhhhhh." ("Time to go.") The wind calls me. I get up and walk.......My path is set. It will take me to the place where dragons awaken. Will I be meeting you there?

—⚬⚬⚬—

"Is this how it all started? Your purpose just got revealed to you by the wind?

Is this how it all started? You just decided to open your mind and become receptive?

Is this how it all started? You dropped all "shoulds" and just followed the "voice"?

Is this how it all started? You stopped judging yourself and surroundings, accepting things as they were?

Is this how it all started? You found a bush in the desert that looked like a sleeping dragon, and it just changed your life?!!!"

"No, it didn't begin in the desert. It couldn't have. If I wasn't prepared to receive this information, I wouldn't have understood the importance of it."

The truth is, it took me another two years to digest the desert experience.

The truth is, it took me another two years to realize the dragon within myself.

The truth is, it took me another two years to understand the mission, the purpose, and meaning it had in my life.

Maybe the dragon felt that the position in which he was sleeping was becoming uncomfortable.

Maybe I felt it stirring, moving.

Maybe it was time to wake up and stretch its wings.

This time of awakening was not the most comfortable period in my human life. Things started shifting, and life started transforming in the most unpredictable manner. I am saying "unpredictable", but I am not completely truthful with myself. I secretly wanted and welcomed the change.

It was a secret. I wouldn't even admit it to myself.

It was a secret, because I was afraid to be judged.

It was a secret, because I was afraid to fall into the darkness of the unknown.

It was a secret, because everything seemed perfect in my life at the time. So how would I justify my urge for a change?

No, I didn't "know" how it would change me. That's why our grandmothers always said, "Be careful of what you wish for." "Yeah-yeah, blah-blah, I heard it a million times before! I know what I am doing."

It's true! I really did know what I was doing. I just didn't know what kind of changes it would bring along. We can anticipate things, but we can never know for sure. Grandmothers specifically used the phrase "what you <u>wish</u> for". They learned through experience that these wishes have magic powers, and "thoughts become things".

My beliefs have changed, or vanished. People I placed on pedestals fell off of them, and new people stepped up. My values were reevaluated, and my lifestyle updated. My sleeping friends preferred to stay asleep, and I had to leave them in the certainty of their comfort zone.

This book is for those:
who feel the yearning for something greater,
who are waking up, or want to awake.
This book is for those
who are lost and confused, yet know,
this is the way to go,
who cannot afford to sleep any longer.
This book is for those
who want to learn who they are,
and what are they here for.
Those who feel that there is more potential or
ability lying dormant within, and who
want to step up to claim their power.

Will I answer all your questions? Maybe. Maybe I won't. I do not pretend to know everything. I don't. I am just a traveler, discovering the secrets of a "Great Desert", just as everyone else is. Some travelers know more than others because they already got to visit the Destination on a journey you are about to embark on. I can tell you for sure, that <u>all the answers you need are already stored within you, but the secret to unlocking them lies in the power of asking the right questions.</u> It is my intent to spark your curiosity, to realize the magnificence of who you are and ways to access it, and to inspire you to continue your journey far beyond this book. I want you to go in search for the truth. I want you to continue learning; I want you to grow and expand. I want you to realize that we are here on this planet for missions other than to collect prizes, drive expensive cars, and live in mansions, although we can enjoy the abundance of it all. I loved my journey, and I am yearning to share with you what I've learned on this path so far.

I thought it might be important to explain the origins of the philosophy behind this book, how it was born. Yet, I also find it very challenging to put a finger on the map, and say, "It began here." As soon as I want to do that, a preceding event pops up in my mind, prompting me to change the beginning of my story to an earlier time. Yet, I understand, that if I follow this impulse of going earlier and earlier, I will depart from the intention of this book further and further, and will have to begin with, "Once upon a time, a girl was born....."

Every event, meeting, conversation,

every book read, tear shed, word said,

every thought released and emotion felt led to the exactly precise moment where I am now and where you are now. Even this meeting between you and me is not a coincidence.

You are holding this book because it has a precise message for you, and you alone.

You are holding this book because the mysterious coincidences in your life, a series of seemingly disconnected events, led you to the exact moment when this book landed itself into your hands.

You are holding this book because it contains the exact answers to the questions you are asking yourself in your life right now. This message is different for every reader. You will learn what your message is all about. Learning ways to receive messages that have importance to you is a special skill that takes practice and an open mind. It becomes the most important signpost, pointing you in the right direction of the next step of your journey.

Allow it to become your Guiding Wind of the Great Desert.

Allow it to take you to your own Bush that looks like a Sleeping Dragon.

Allow yourself to recognize it!

Allow it to become a catalyst for awakening the Sleeping Dragon within you.

—⟨∿∿⟩—

1

The Music

Choreographer's Guiding Principals

"Music gives a soul to the universe, wings to the mind, flight to the imagination and life to everything."

~ Plato

1

The Music

Choreographer's Guiding Principals

" Okay, we are done. I am ready. Thank you," said Sasha as she left the ice. February 10, 2006, it was a beautiful, warm, and sunny Friday morning. In a few hours she would be relaxing in the airplane, leaving me, this rink, and her home in California behind, en route to Turin, Italy, where in 11 days she would be representing United States in the 2006 Olympics. She'd come to the rink to see me for a last quick tune-up lesson, a small reassurance, and a boost of confidence just before heading off to LAX. We were done, and I felt sad that she was leaving. I was anticipating the return of my "normal" life, where there was no Sasha, to the life of coaching young Olympic hopefuls, who would take many long years of training to ripen. I hoped to become an Olympic coach one day in my own right, as the main coach of an athlete. But for now I was here to say the last words of encouragement and "good luck", then disappear into the gray-uneventful-sameness of everyday living...

I watched her from a distance sitting on the bench in the spacious lobby, bending over to unlace her skates. Small and delicate, she seemed completely absorbed by her task. I walked towards her, mentally rehearsing my prepared "good luck" speech. I took a breath to begin my pep talk, but she interjected:

"Could you do me a favor, and meet me in Italy tomorrow?"

I was startled. "Oooookaaay." That was definitely not something I expected, not a few hours before her plane departed. Sure, people asked me all the time if I was going to travel with her. But she had never asked, not until now, anyway.

Sasha and I had worked quite a bit together. I helped with her training and provided additional emotional support, especially when things were less than perfect. She was traveling with her mom and a long-time coach John Nicks, and my presence was not necessary. Her question unnerved me. It was one of those things I wasn't prepared for. I called my husband with the news and an urgent request to book a flight to Geneva for me.

It was a frantic, hurried preparation for travel, but two days later I was in Italy, ready for the final week of Sasha's training high in the Italian Alps at the rink designated by the U.S. Figure Skating Association for their skaters.

We stayed in a small, picturesque town of Courmayeur on the Italian side of Mount Mont Blanc. The rink was gorgeous, resembling more of a chapel than the athletic training facility. Beautiful sun rays penetrated the huge Gothic-styled stained-glass window, reflecting multicolored sunlight spots on the freshly resurfaced ice. The back wall was covered by a gigantic photo-mural of the Snowy Alps, creating a feel of skating outdoors. It was sunny and bright. Sasha skated there for two hours in the morning and two hours in the evening. In between training sessions, she took naps or just rested in the mountain chalet-styled hotel room, warm and cozy, watching TV or reading a book, while I took walks in town with her mother Galina. It was a fascinating time.

I became really good friends with Galina, and she told me captivating stories about Sasha, her previous training, life, etc. We also discussed how the preparation for the competition was going and what we could do to maximize it.

It was then that Galina shared with me about one of Sasha's coaches who had an incredible influence on their lives. It sounded like they had a lot of respect for this man, and Sasha called him a few times for advice while we were in Courmayeur. I was slightly irritated by the fact that both myself and Mr. Nicks were available for help, yet she was calling this other person in Russia for advice. This coach had not seen her in a long time; what could he possibly help her with? However, it spiked my interest! I wanted to know more about this man. What did he have or know that called for such command and respect?! What was so special about him? What was his secret? Galina told me unbelievable things about this man's healing and intuitive abilities. I had a difficult time accepting the fact that there was someone, a coach, who conceived something I knew nothing about. In fact, what I heard from Galina sounded more like science fiction or fairy tale than reality. I found it very mysterious and intriguing. It was then that I decided for myself that I would develop these abilities as well, if there really was such a thing. The seed got planted. Like all seeds, it took time to germinate and sprout, and I actually forgot about it for a while, until one day two years later, I wandered into Barnes and Nobles and a book called *The Way of the Peaceful Warrior* got my attention. I picked it up.

—◦∕∕∕◦—

The cover of this book had a photograph of a half-naked man hanging upside down with arms open in a V shape and a sign underneath soliciting the reader with the cheesy headline, "A Book That Changes Lives". Even now I am not sure what prompted me to leave the store with that book. It was the end of December 2008, time of winter break. By then I was a first-year student of the master's program in Applied Sports Psychology. I felt free to read whatever I wanted, and this book took an honorary position of becoming my official reading material for vacation. As I journeyed deeper into the story of world-class gymnast Dan and his odd teacher Socrates, I started feeling a light mixture of excitement and anxiety. I felt like I knew about Socrates from somewhere, and he was going to play an important part in my life. Socrates was matching the description of the coach Sasha's mother Galina told me about. Now I was certain that what she told me about their coach was not a fantasy. People with "magical" abilities existed. Moreover, these abilities were stored within every human, and it was our choice to awaken to them. I imagined the opening to the world of possibilities if I unlocked these skills and taught them to my students! But first, I had to figure out where I could learn these skills. Where could I find my Socrates who was willing to teach me that? The book didn't have a map, and the only direction it gave was a reassurance that I, too, have these abilities, and somehow I will discover the way to unlock them.

In February 2009 I took my first yoga and meditation class. In that class we were shown a couple of breathing exercises and a special gaze. I remember the thrill I felt the next day as I taught my students to do these exercises on the ice. In a matter of minutes they evolved into beautiful angels that came down from one of Michelangelo's frescoes. Their skating transformed, and they appeared floating above the ice, effortless in their movement, transparent in their appearance. In that instant I knew that Michelangelo, too, saw and experienced the same angels I did. From that day on, I was certain that I was on to something very special. Everyone knew it. I did; all of the kids did; and all of the parents observing from the stands knew it. It was breathtaking. However, very quickly I realized that even though I'd tapped into something magnificent, I was yet to discover what it was or how to tap into it on a consistent basis, especially in competitions. I also knew that I'd hit the point of no return on that day. I couldn't continue teaching skating the same old way anymore.

Choreography of Awakening was largely born of the discoveries I have made since that memorable day over five years ago when my skaters turned into the angels. Many of these "discoveries" I have formulated and successfully applied in teaching my students long before I took this journey. These "inspirations" worked magic, and the accolades and medals that my students have won on national and international levels spoke volumes of its potency. However, it wasn't until later that I understood the extent and depth of what I was teaching, why it worked, and what it meant. Nevertheless, I felt affirmed and proud that I had invented a "wheel" all by myself. It didn't bother me that my discovery really came into existence almost 3000 years ago and possibly even before that! I am not insisting that what you are reading here is original and new. It is as old as civilization itself. However, what you are reading here is <u>my</u> expression of the Wisdoms of Ages, the way I understood and applied them to my life. What you are reading here, I have successfully taught to my students and clients, and I firmly believe that you, too, can benefit from these teachings......

Over five years have passed since the day I witnessed my students disappearing as "skaters" and coming forth as skating angels.

Today I was reminded of one of those "magic moments" that became the reason behind writing this chapter.

Today I again attended the Tao study class where we read and discussed the little book full of wisdom, *Tao te Ching*.

Today again I heard the magic words of ancient Chinese sage Lao Tzu, filled with beauty and poetry, perfectly describing my ice angels 2800 years ago, as if he had seen them with his own eyes:

> *"The ancient Masters were profound and subtle.*
> *Their wisdom was unfathomable.*
> *There was no way to describe it;*
> *all we can describe is their appearance.*
> *They were careful*
> *as someone crossing an iced-over stream.*
> *Alert as a warrior in enemy territory.*
> *Courteous as a guest.*
> *Fluid as melting ice.*
> *Shapable as a block of wood.*
> *Receptive as a valley.*
> *Clear as a glass of water..."*

Something jumped inside of me as I was hearing and reading these words. They sounded like perfect music. My heart rejoiced. Yes! My angels are so perfectly set forth. And just like that, I had found the perfect choreographer's philosophy: Tao.

2

<u>Opening Pose</u>

Clean Slate

"I learned how essential it is to be willing to let go of anything I think I know in service to discovering something I don't know."

~Ron and Mary Hulnick

2

Opening Pose

Clean Slate

I began coaching as a 20-year-old innocent, naive beginner. I didn't know anything about coaching, skating in the United States, rules, competitions, seminars, conferences, skating federations, or ice shows. We were newly arrived immigrants from the Soviet Union, residing in New York City, trying to figure out the American way of living, the English language, and simply explore the job market available for people like us. We were literally trying to survive in the land of opportunities. One day fate brought me to the Rockefeller Center, prompted me to put the skates on, and skate. It felt really good. I always enjoyed skating outdoors. It reminded me of skating with my dad on the frozen lakes in Russia; cold air caressing my cheeks, the sound of the cracking ice, and an adrenaline rush warning me of the dangers skating on the lakes. The reassuring smile of my dad prompted me to move forward. I was completely absorbed in my experience and memories, and unaware that someone was watching me.

His name was Martin, and he worked as a skate guard at the Rockefeller Center's ice rink. He was a big African-American guy, wearing a Mets baseball hat, oversized heather sweatshirt, and baggy jeans. Perhaps he used to be a hockey skater, but now he was in charge of the skaters' safety during public sessions. I stood out from the crowd and immediately drew his interest. He approached me and started a conversation about my skating, my accent, our whereabouts, and life. Then he asked me casually if I was interested in working at an ice rink. Of course I was! It was an opportunity to leisurely stroll around the rink and get paid for it! It was an opportunity to do something that was fun and to quit my cleaning job and still be able to help my parents with the expenses. It promised to be a perfect marriage of part-time job and entertainment!

As soon as the session was over, we took our skates off and Martin immediately escorted me to another ice rink several blocks down the road, deceptively located in the penthouse of an office building. I was hired on the spot, and began working at the ice rink the very next day. I can confidently say now that meeting Martin that day changed the course of my life, and this book is a direct result of it. It's funny that I have just now remembered his name and what he looked like, even though I must have seen him only once or twice in my life, more than 20 years ago.

I became a skate guard at the Sky Rink in New York City. Very soon I made friends with other skate guards, and charmed them with my skating abilities. They started urging me to audition for skating shows and begin teaching little kids. I easily yielded to their persuasion, and boldly, if not recklessly, embarked on the skating path. Reckless and bold because I didn't know what I was doing, or where I was going. I had no plan and didn't take much time to analyze my options or think through my decisions. I lived in the moment and was open to an opportunity as it presented itself. I didn't know how to teach skating or even where to begin. I didn't even know the names of the skating elements in English. Yet, I was excited, enthusiastic, and full of optimism.

With abandon, I let my (skate guard) friends take me to an audition for Disney on Ice tour company. It went very well, and the Disney people told me, "We'll contact you," or so I heard them say! I was so excited. I loved performing and traveling, and here I had an opportunity to do both. This promised to be so much better than studying boring accounting at Brooklyn College.

Yes, that's right! I was being groomed to be an accountant, as a diligent and obedient daughter of a Russian-Jewish immigrant family. Like thousands of other immigrant boys and girls who became accountants, programmers, doctors, lawyers, pharmacists, and dentists. For a child of an immigrant, choosing a degree at the university was not a question of love and passion, but a question of survival and making a living.

I pretty much quit going to college then while waiting for my "tour" with Disney on Ice to begin. I worked at the rink during the day, and every evening I checked my mailbox for the Disney-stamped envelope. I listened carefully to every voicemail on my phone. But the mail was slow, and the message I was expecting was taking forever to arrive. Then one day my phone rang. My heart skipped a beat, as I could just sense that my skating dream was about to be realized. I picked up the receiver, and on the other end was the voice of my boyfriend, suggesting that I get a degree in coaching figure skating. I was disappointed, and I argued the impossibility of his proposal. Eventually I learned that indeed the University of Delaware did offer such a degree, and I was soon on my way to earn it.

Looking back, I see this 19-year-old girl taking a leap of faith, leaving her family behind, moving to a different state all by herself. She barely had any knowledge of the English language. She had no job, no security, no money, and no clue how she would pay for school, much less her food. Her parents could not support her at all. They were barely surviving themselves; learning English, new professions, and taking care of my little sister.

Sometimes today I face difficult decisions, standing at the crossroads of, where should I go from here? Should I continue carrying on my life as is or go for something different, challenging myself to step up and evolve? Many people arrive at these crossroads wavering, unable to step forward, afraid. What are they afraid of? What am I afraid of?

My situation today is so much better than it was then when I was 19. I fluently speak, write, and teach in English. I am educated and credentialed. A Google search of my name provides a long list of my accomplishments, and I harbor full support and security from my family. What do I have to be afraid of now? What is the difference between the accomplished, successful, educated, poised 41-year-old woman and a naive 19-year-old youth?

At 19, I was a BEGINNER, unaware of the dangers of life, a simple-minded beginner!

At 19, I never saw the possibility of failure. In fact, my English vocabulary was so poor that it didn't even contain the word "failure"!

At 19, I was absolutely certain of my success!

At 19, I had complete, unfailing confidence in myself, and in my ability to figure things out!

At 19, I *"had nothing, thus had nothing to lose."**

But as I was learning more, wanting more, getting more, I gained success, knowledge, money, and....fear, fear of losing that which I had achieved. I became an expert in fear.

> *"In the beginner's mind there are many possibilities;*
> *in the expert's mind there are few."*
> ~S. Suzuki

As we move through life, winning and losing, trusting and being betrayed, loving and getting rejected, trying and being unappreciated, opening up and being laughed at, we become guarded, hardened, closed-minded, and closed-hearted. Maybe that's what happened to Adam and Eve when they were expelled from Paradise for tasting the fruit of the Knowledge Tree. Although, I don't believe that they were "expelled", but I do believe that they lost their inner Eden, which was the innocence, peacefulness, and centeredness of the mind. Buddhists call it the "Beginner's Mind".

When I first entered the waters of coaching, I knew nothing. My cup was empty, and I was ambitious and eager to fill it up. I was learning techniques from some of the best coaches in the world. I was learning the sports sciences of biomechanics, physiology, anatomy, and psychology from the professors having direct experience with elite figure skaters. I was learning injury prevention, strength and conditioning techniques, nutrition, and theater; you name it! My energy was limitless. I was everywhere where I could learn something. This hunger for knowledge was the driving force behind my successfulness. Yet, with each success I accomplished, my ego, like an empire, was growing larger and more guarded. My cup was getting fuller. My motivation to learn shifted gears from "I love learning" to "I need to know more than my competitors, have better skills, more credentials." It shifted from excitement of a curious youth, to a fear-based, necessity-oriented learning of an adult.

But one day, I will come across a quote in a book, and I will change my mind about how I should approach learning. It will help me to <u>consciously</u> return to and embrace the wisdom of my 19-year-old beginner self, and embark on a completely new path....But it will happen later...

...I picture a young child playing with a toy; a doll, a truck, a car. She is completely absorbed in the process, moving the toy from place to place, talking to it, making funny sounds. Then suddenly, she becomes quiet. In this moment she discovers that there is more to the toy than the naked eye can see. She discovers that by pulling a piece apart, a whole new world filled with possibilities opens up inside the toy. She discovers a whole new game behind the facade. She breaks the truck. She rips Barbie's head off and picks inside her head and her body. She puts a piece of the toy in her mouth and bites on it. She wants to know her toy, inside and out. Is it empty? Is it full? What does it taste like? Why do the parts move the way they do? She then tries to put it back together, all the while trying to learn how it works.

For a while, coaching skating was my toy. I played with it. I loved it! It was one of the most fun toys I ever had in my life! I learned all the techniques, how the elements work; rules, programs, competitions, workouts. Someone could say that I achieved an incredible level of success, but I couldn't acknowledge it. I always had a sense not being good enough. I always worried about somebody else being better than me, not being approved by my clients, parents, peers, officials...

(I am 7)

...My mother demanding perfection of every letter written. She is reading my workbook like a hawk, searching for mistakes. If she finds one, I'll be punished. If not, I'll be spared this time. Her love and approval depends on the quality of work I produce. I am in first grade, but I know, getting a 'B' is not an option. I cannot embarrass my mother. I can only have 'A's and do well in competitions so that she can tell her friends about my successes. Then my butt can be spared, and maybe I can even have a hug....

(I am 37)

"What place did she get?" My mother wants to know what place my student got at competition.

"Second," I respond.

"What?" she yells into the receiver, unable to comprehend and hear that there are places other than 'first' that exist out there.

"Second, she got second!" I am irritated.

"Oh.....Why only second?" She is disappointed. "Second" is not good enough. I am not "good enough". The level of my "goodness" is measured by the accomplishments of my students. I must find the way to be better, so much better, that my students will never be "second" again, and I will finally find peace and a sense of completeness.

I rip Barbie's head off. I look inside. And there I see a dark emptiness. There is nothing inside this Barbie. She is un-filled and hollow. She is just a plastic form. I realize, that this is the reason behind our discontent, behind my discontent. We are hollow and empty. We are trying to fulfill this vacuum inside of us by filling the space around us! New cars, homes, Chanel bags, Gucci shoes, Mikimoto pearls. I have it all, but I am still empty, as empty as this Barbie doll. But is this void free from substance? Is it really empty? Don't our emotions and thoughts come from it? As a figure skating coach, I trained bodies to be in perfect shape and form, but I realized that a tiny whiff of emotion could ruin a whole year of training and hard work. Where are these emotions coming from? I started learning about psychology in hopes of filling the gaps. I picked up a few effective techniques to control thoughts and emotions under stressful conditions and taught them to my students. The results were almost immediate, and I felt reassured that I'd stepped in the right direction.

The seed planted in Turin had begun sprouting.

I became excited at the proposition that I had found a secret formula to success. I decided to enter the masters program in Applied Sports Psychology to get a diploma that would validate and prove to the whole world that I KNOW THE SECRET!!!! I began my studies with an attitude of an expert, knowing more than my professor. My professor, after all, was just a man in the university who was doing research and teaching psychology from the textbooks. He was not applying the methods to his athletes' training, preparing them for the events, watching them compete and win. I was doing that.

My results were proven. My method was working. All I needed now was a certificate to seal and validate this knowledge. My professor was patient. He must have met many arrogant, ego-driven people, who believed that they knew it all. Yet they were hollow and unfulfilled inside, people who lost their beginner's mind and the blissful happiness of a child, all to chase success, money, power, and recognition.

So many of us fall into this trap. My wise professor wasn't arguing, pushing, or debating. He was observing and assigning textbooks, facilitating learning and understanding, understanding of our minds. And then it happened! It was then I came across the quote in one of my textbooks that transformed my view of learning. In one instant everything came to the center of clarity and opened a floodgate to "empty the cup" and to accept the knowledge in a different way, to embrace the beginner's mind all over again. This whole chapter is really dedicated to this quote. When I read it to my daughter Abbie, the innocence in her wondered, "It is so simple! Why would you need to write so many pages about it?" I don't know. Maybe because it took so many years to arrive at the simplicity of this concept. Here it is:

"Objects of knowledge are like water that has become ice and prevents the river from flowing. We need knowledge, but we have to use it intelligently. When we think that our present knowledge is paramount, our way ahead is blocked. Our knowledge has become an obstacle."
~Thich Nhat Hanh

Then I realized that the body and all the material that we can see, taste, feel, and touch are just the visible small part of an iceberg. 'Under the dark blue of the ocean,' invisible to the eyes, lies the vast part of the true nature of this beast, virgin in its undiscovered solitude, hiding its great mysteries and powers, and untapped into potentials. I realized, that it is our birthright to grow, learn, and evolve. That is the reason and goal for our being: to awaken to the Presence of our Soul and its desire to know itself! To become conscious co-creators of the Universe, and to claim our right to be happy and fulfilled, to be whole! I realized that to awaken our awareness to it, we must evoke our beginner's mind, and embark on the journey of diving into the puzzlement of the murky emptiness of our inner self, our subconscious mind, and embrace and surrender to our fears. The time has come to recognize and accept the nature of our infinite potential.

OPENING POSE PRACTICE

To assist you in anchoring what you've learned, I'd like to invite you to take a pen and a journal and find a comfortable place to sit where you won't be disturbed. Reflect on your thoughts and understanding of the Beginner's Mind concept.

- Recall the most recent time in your life when you shut down and decided that you already knew what the person had to say, or where you judged them as incompetent. If you had an opportunity to be in this situation again, what could you have learned?

- How could you benefit in your life, relationship, job, if you chose to open your mind to new ideas?

- For the next week practice listening to people as if you have never heard them before. Imagine hearing their soul with the ears of your soul. What was this experience like?

3

The Theme

Answering the Call

"When you are inspired by some great purpose, some extraordinary project, all your thoughts break their bonds: Your mind transcends limitations, your consciousness expands in every direction, and you find yourself in a new, great, and wonderful world. Dormant forces, faculties and talents become alive, and you discover yourself to be a greater person by far than you ever dreamed yourself to be."

~Patanjali, 150 B.C.

3

The Theme

Answering the Call

Saturday morning, and I was preparing for my friend's visit. As I ran through the house making sure that everything was in pristine condition, I somewhat worried, what are we going to talk about? What could be a theme for our conversation? What is a definition of a theme? I reached for the dictionary and looked up synonyms: substance, phenomenon, matter, and then meaning, or intention and purpose. As a choreographer, I always had to decide on the theme first, then the story. What emotions do I want to evoke in my audience? What thoughts do I want to provoke in them? I always strived to create programs with a purpose and a deeper meaning, and felt that without a theme, they turned into a meaningless set of elements. It didn't occur to me before, that our lives are just like the skater's programs and require a theme, or meaning, and purpose.

"Perhaps our conversation would revolve around this subject," I thought, and before I knew it, my mind started an internal dialogue with my friend, speaking in voices, one for me and one for her, one asking, the other responding.

We've known each other for a long time. Her daughter is a successful skater, and my former student. A few years ago our paths divided and we went different ways. For a while the split had caused a sense of disconnect and detachment between us. Yet, in the time apart, we discovered that not only did we still have genuine affinity towards each other, but surprisingly, we grew closer in our understanding of the world.

In my inner conversation with her, I reflected upon the time when I believed that it was my destiny and purpose to be a figure skating coach. Perhaps I was misinterpreting the context between destiny and purpose. I've since discovered that the 'thing you do' (coaching skating in my case) is just an element in the program we call Life, as well as an effective tool towards the revelation of one's mission, but not the mission itself.

"What about you?" I silently asked my friend. "What did you unearth during the time we were apart? Playing the role of a mother of a competitive skater is not a simple task: juggling normal family obligations, rigors of the competitive athlete's life, and personal aspirations."

In my mind's eye I saw her daily struggles with doubts as she was watching her girl practicing, sensitive to every mistake and hurting for every fall. Was she doing the right thing for her baby, herself, and her family?

I began to think of all her sacrifices, dreams, disappointments, long lapses of time devoid of any visible progress and even the appearance of moving backwards, wondering where this was all going. Surely, she was aware of many disillusioned mothers freezing their butts and draining their family's savings at ice rinks across the world. All of them dreaming of their talented daughters catching a moment of stardom, then losing all in the chase, sometimes even the relationships with their daughters for whom they sacrificed their youthful years of life. What makes her and her daughter different? Would she be able to endure, or lose patience and face the fate of many other skating moms who lost this battle?

Only recently I was struck with the realization that becoming a champion in sports also couldn't be a purpose or mission in itself, but it can become a great platform to spring from towards the discovery of one's potential, one's true essence, and the application of it for the greater good.

I remembered many conversations I had with parents, skaters, and coaches in the locker rooms, casually chatting about what was truly important, yet they were quick to forget about these values in the heat of the race for more trophies, titles, power, significance, or prestige....

...This race had always begun with an innocent aspiration of winning Regionals. A small taste of victory was all they had ever wanted. Driven parents; obedient, hard-working children; and ambitious coaches were willingly pushing themselves towards their goals, disregarding freezing predawn practice hours, long commutes to the rinks, and considerable investments in every realm of human existence.

And finally, the coveted position on the podium had been conquered and a medal of honor awarded. Yet it arrived with the sweet, luring song of an invisible Siren whispering quietly into the yet-uncorrupt ear:

"It is too early to be happy," she warned. "The game is on you. You must prepare for Sectionals. You'll celebrate thereafter! Imagine, the happiness you'll feel winning that!" Siren entices, "Come on! One more push, you are almost there!"

A little itch raised up just a notch, a tiny spark of anxiety and pressure. Logic was in an agreement with the Siren. "This is a sport, and there is nothing wrong with the desire to win Sectionals. The Siren is right. We need to crank up a bit more intensity. We have a chance!"

Sectionals came along, and....

..Another victory revealed benevolence of gods.

Intoxicating!

Yet there was no time to celebrate triumph.

A long-held breath was now released, "Phew. At once we REALLY know what would bring us satisfaction and fulfillment: the win at Nationals!" "That's right!" echoes the Siren.

"Sectionals are really not that important, if you think about it. Nationals is a whole new game plan!" They hear her, and begin to pray, work, dream, sacrifice more to the altar of the skating god. He's auspicious and grants their wish, yet holds them in his vigilance.

They basked in the moment of glory and excitement, threw in a party in celebration, and pampered the victor! But before long, the Siren had returned. She learned her way into their heads, earned their trust, and gained power. She could speak in their own voices:

"I am a national champion. I have to prove that I'm worth it.... that I can improve.... that I am better than 'Joneses'. The 'Smiths', in second place, should not catch me next year..." The rat race began. The ever-hungry Siren wants more and never has enough. Her appetite proves bottomless, and her attitude is mean. She demands more wins but gives no fulfillment in return. She only brings relief. Dare to lose and she brings the agony. Practices are now filled with constant anxieties and worries. They end up in injuries, eating disorders, broken families, and depression.

I was one of those ambitious coaches. I coached a few of those obedient, hard-working students and conspired with their driven parents. I've met the 'Siren' on more than one occasion. I got to know her well after spending years of listening to her lies and promises, until I woke up...

I remember a few years back reading a book written by Rudolf Zagaynov, a famous sports psychologist of many

Russian elite athletes, including Alexei Yagudin, 2002 Olympic Champion. This man had an aura of mystery surrounding him and his unique abilities to put athletes in the zone, to inspire them to reach further into their potential, to go for that that seemed impossible. I was completely sold on his expertise, and wanted to learn about his 'magic formulas.' Zagaynov's book *What For?* surprised me. It began with an icy-cold yet heart-wrenching description of a cafeteria in the Olympic village, filled with spent athletes at the end of the day.

"I could clearly identify men who lost by their motionless gaze, infantile confusion, incomprehension of the situation, pitiful resignation to the circumstances, and heart-broken women with red, swollen-from-tears eyes." Wrote Zagaynov. "But what surprised me was the fact that I couldn't differentiate the faces of the champions. They didn't reflect the joy of victory, triumph of realization of one's dream as one would expect. Yes, the face of a newly born Olympic champion mirrored back fatigue, emotional and physical devastation, and withdrawal."

I remember the confusion I felt reading these lines. I couldn't grasp it. How could one be in low spirits after reaching his dream? I worked relentlessly every day for 20 years pulled by the dancing vision in my mind: coach champions. I was convinced then that I would be ecstatic if my hopes materialized! This man didn't know what he was talking about! However, as I experienced later, he did know what he was talking about, and his words echoed almost exactly the words of a famous American author, Dr. Stephen Covey:

> *"People often find themselves achieving victories that are empty, successes that have come at the expense of things they suddenly realize were far more valuable to them. People from every walk of life—doctors, academicians, actors, politicians, business professionals, athletes, and plumbers—often struggle to achieve a higher income, more recognition, or a certain degree of professional competence, only to find that their drive to achieve their goal blinded them to the things that really mattered most and now are gone."*

Zagaynov's book was written in Russian, and I, a native Russian speaker educated in English, was going back and forth translating the concepts he was describing in Russian into the philosophy I adapted to in English. *"What For?"* had a depressing tendency, not at all what I was looking for. I was searching for the inspiration, for the meaning, for the explanation of, 'Why do I want to do what I do so much?' And then I found it, in the middle of the book, seemingly not connected to anything he wrote:

> *"The most important thing that a human must have in his life and in his life's work is purpose! When I see an athlete with the special glare in his eyes before the game begins, I know that he is going into the battle for a reason. Today he is absolutely inspired by his purpose and his mission, and today he is ready to give it all in the act of faith"*

That's it! I was waiting for this quote! I was looking for it. I was confused for a while by the title *What for?* It didn't sound quite right. It sounded more like questioning, "What did I waste my entire life for?", here it was, a question of WHY? It was one of the "aha" moments, when suddenly you know. Ask yourself **"Why?"** <u>before</u> you begin, and keep checking yourself as you go, then you won't have to ask yourself **"What for?"** <u>after</u> you are done.

My friend would be arriving shortly, and while waiting for her, I continued our silent conversation:

"Hey, your daughter is still young. There is a great opportunity to establish the 'Big Why' now, before it's too late, before both of you become the Siren's pray and get sucked into her game. You have no idea how often I've been brushed off as a naive romantic and told something like this: "Of course, we understand what you are saying. But we feel that right now our daughter lacks her technical skills to be a strong, high-level competitor. Our coaches concur that is the case and that she will not make it to the international level until she gets her jumps. There is quite a bit more pressure and expectation from others now that she is a national competitor and on a team envelope, and so that is what we need to focus on." And then, before you know it, they are gone from the sport in complete disillusion, asking themselves that dreaded question, "What for?""

"Why?" you might ask.

"Many reasons: burnout, injuries, lack of progress, politics, who knows!" So many super-talented athletes disappear. As your friend, I so hope that this will not become your path and that you would recognize the Siren's voice when she starts whispering into your ear! She is a master in planting fear in people's heads, blocking the voice of their hearts and zapping their energy, or perhaps loaning the energy, then withdrawing it with a huge interest, leaving you completely 'bankrupt.'

Satisfying "other's expectations" and responding to "pressure" is her not-so-subtle way of eating away your joy and love for doing what you do. She is using fear as a source of energy and motivation. Fear can be a powerful motivator. That's why many coaches, parents, bosses, spouses, politicians, religions use it to manipulate those in their care into doing things they might not have done otherwise. Fear-based work produces quick results, and the Siren knows that, but she is not after the results. Her food is your energy, and once she has what she wants, you'll be left empty, drained, disillusioned, burned out, asking yourself "What for?" The sooner you realize the 'true source' of your power, the better your chances to 'survive.' Your limitless potential is locked in the answer of the 'Big Why' question. It is a source of inspiration found in high purpose, in a selfless service or a contribution to some cause. Every mother instinctively knows that as she is serving her child, loving him unconditionally."

"Abbie." I turned towards my daughter who was lingering around me, "tell me, why do you want to become a singer?" She gave me a serious, thoughtful look before responding. "Well, I want to bring joy and happiness to my listeners. I want to in-spire them, but also, singing brings joy to me." I chuckled; she still knows the right answer. Hopefully, I'll be able to guard her innocence from hungry Sirens as she grows older.

Suddenly my thoughts shifted to the meeting I recent-ly had with a past student, now a UCLA graduate: Angelyn Nguyen. Angelyn chose to stop skating a few years ago in favor of attending school full time. She was a talented skater who devoted many years of life to honing her skills. She attained a considerable level of success and was on her way up to be-come a national-level competitor. Upon her decision to move on with her life, I felt that she was cutting ties with the sport too soon, never realizing the depth of her potential. When she called me for lunch, I secretly hoped that she wanted to come back to the sport, to accomplish that which she had given up upon. But as we spoke, I realized that her intention of seeing me was to express gratitude for the skills I taught her, for the mental skills she was still using daily in her life. Angelyn wanted to reassure me that she had never really "stopped skating." She just merely changed the choreography of her "Program" and the names of the elements it contained. Biochemistry became her double Axel, and biology her triple Salchow. Exams became her competitions, and homework her practice. As she was talk-ing about her chosen field of study and of the decision she made to enter a graduate Ph.D. program, she was expressing happiness, joy, and love for what she was doing and conviction in the rightness of her choice. Her eyes were shining brightly, and her speech was elevated, indicating high levels of energy. Very soon my feelings of her unfulfilled path of self-discovery in skating faded away and gave way to excitement and certainty that she was in her element and never quit anything. Intuitively she sensed that becoming a national competitor and winning medals would have been a pleasurable but meaningless experience as her heart was set on devoting itself to explorations in science. While some people were feeling sorry for her decision to part with the sport, she was affirming that life has many ways to fulfill the purpose and the mission we are here for. Wise beyond her years, Angelyn has recognized the valuable tool that skating was for her, a tool that not only expanded her awareness of herself but taught her the necessary skills needed to progress towards the next level of mastery.

I thought about how many people get stuck doing what they no longer believe in. Some of them continue dragging on in fear of being perceived as losers or failures should they choose to make a change. Others get lost in the "What for?" question and now are afraid to make any move, terrified of another "What for?" How many become so numb that they can't hear the calling of their Souls; resigned - they are dragging their lives as mules towing their heavy loads? Our society, obsessed with winning, promotes such slogans as

"Winners never quit, and quitters never win,"

and fails to recognize the true purpose of our being: growth, expansion, and contribution, the awakening and unfolding of the Sleeping Dragon. Who is this giant, and what does he need? If he can't fit into his old suit any longer, isn't it time to change it, to redefine the mission, to pinpoint his passion? That change will take place regardless of his mind's wishes to remain. The question is, which direction will this change take? Will it follow the path of self-distraction towards depression and addictions or a path of expansion towards self-realization? I felt so inspired by the Angelyn's courage to follow her heart and discover the new purpose despite the inner and outer pressure she felt to remain where she was, just because she had skated for so long and was good at it.

A signal coming from my iPhone interrupted my thoughts on the theme of "Life's Purpose." I looked on the caller ID. My friend was letting me know that she was 10 minutes away. I was ready for her. "What can I do during these 10 minutes?" Facebook! A perfect distraction and time killer. I opened my computer, and in a few seconds I was logged into the biggest social media network in the world with its famous blue page. A post called for my attention, written by a skater, Wesley Campbell:

"22 years of skating. The only place I call home is the ice. We train, prepare, dream, achieve. Today is about the art. The heart and soul of everything that I know to be true about myself. I am an artist. I will never be the national champion in men's singles, but no one can take away my joy. I will leave my heart out there today, and give this gift to God, the audience, and myself. I will leave Omaha

loving skating. And move forward with joy in my heart. Today is a day for celebration."

I read the post and grasped for the air. In one short paragraph Wesley expressed all my thoughts and emotions. I felt my heart opening to receive his offering of love, even though I haven't seen him skate yet. I realized that he wrote this as an intention, a sort of a prayer, before stepping on the ice to skate his long program at U.S. Nationals for the last time. He decided to retire from competition and move on with his life. His message was carrying so much loving energy and power in its authenticity that I wondered about the possibilities opening up for him. I reread the post a few more times, as if I wanted to commit to memory every word of it, then closed my eyes and sent him my prayers.

Wesley was in 20th place after completing the first segment of the championship, the Short Program, in a deep field of the best U.S. men competing for the championship title. It was true that Campbell had no chance of scoring a medal, yet I had a feeling that something magical was going to happen during his Long Program.

When later in the day I checked the results of the Championship Men's event, Wesley succeeded in moving up to 11th place in the Long Program. But the placement on paper didn't really tell the whole story, and I anxiously waited for the videos to be posted on Icenetwork.com. I had to watch him perform with my own eyes, and finally I did.

His body, through the language of movement, communicated the very same intention he put out earlier on Facebook. He appeared to be in a sacred communion with the Divine. It was not skating that anyone knew, or perhaps he became the skating himself. It really didn't matter what place he took or points amassed because what he got was immeasurably more than any competition placement could offer. And just as an affirmation to my own impressions, an article appeared in the Figure Skating: From the Boards blog:

"Wesley Campbell, skating in his fourth U.S. Championships, stopped at center ice, took a breath, and for the next four and a half minutes, it was as if he was painting the perfect picture to compliment each note of "Ave Maria" as it filled the arena. It was as if no one dared breathe for fear of breaking the spell. No one dared blink for fear of missing a second of the magic. He checked off triple jumps like they were as natural as breathing. It was a moment so brilliant it brought the crowd to its feet. Everyone in the building knew they had witnessed the fulfilling of a dream. Medals and scores were irrelevant. The satisfaction of living up to the potential of the moment was more than enough."

FINDING THE THEME
FOR YOUR PROGRAM

In the following exercise I invite you to take a deep look inside yourself. One way of becoming aware of your purpose is to understand yourself.

- Write down the names of three or four people who have inspired you through the course of your life. They could be real people or fictional characters.
- What was their purpose?
- Is there a common thread about these people? What is it? What does it have to do with you?
- What are your values? Do you live your life in alignment with your values?
- How would your life change if you did?

4
Footwork, Steps and Transitions

On the Wings of Inspiration

"Inspiration is when an idea gets hold of you and you feel compelled to let that impulse or energy carry you along. You get to a point where you realize that you're no longer in charge, that there's a driving force inside you that can't be stopped."

~ Wayne Dyer

4

Footwork, Steps
and Transitions

On the Wings of Inspiration

"*Hey! I have a question/favor to ask of you....do you mind filling out a letter of recommendation form for me? It's to get into the Athletic Training program at BYU. Let me know if you can. I miss you. Hope you are well!!*" read a text message on my iPhone. I was resting, sitting on the rock some 8500 feet high in the San Jacinto Mountains, breathing hard, slightly light-headed. There was no time to acclimate to the altitude in a rapid 6000-foot tram ascent. I was watching my husband and daughter climbing a huge boulder in front of me when I felt the vibration of my phone. I was surprised that the phone detected a signal there. I picked it up and looked on the caller ID. Whoa! Deanna Inn, my former student!

I coached Deanna for eight years, from the time she was an awkward, skinny little eight-year-old, barely learning her single jumps, till she was a competitive Novice-level skater at 16. Along the way, she made two trips to Junior Nationals, placing an honorable fourth in Intermediate Ladies, and another trip to Pacific Coast Sectionals, where she became a first alternate to U.S. Nationals. A chronic knee injury forced her to stop skating. Now, she is a student in the university, and a coach. She coaches figure skating.

"Dear Dr. XYZ,

It is my privilege and honor to recommend Deanna Inn for the Athletic Training Educational Program..." I wrote once I got home from the mountains. As I continued to write this letter, I was swept by the memories of our time together, long hours of training, intense moments of competitions, hopes, dreams, lessons, and learnings, Switzerland, chocolate medals.... What did I teach her? What did she teach me? I was overwhelmed by the gratitude for taking this trip into the past, to remember, to appreciate, to experience it all over again.

"In conclusion, I want to reiterate that I highly recommend this dedicated, talented young lady for the admission to ATEP. She is truly positioned very well to make a meaningful contribution. If you have any additional questions, please contact me at your convenience." Period. Letter is

finished and is ready to be mailed. I paused, reread it from the beginning, printed it, and put it in the envelope, then wrote an email to Deanna.

> *"Hey!*
> *I mailed the letter today. Attached is a copy.*
> *Good luck with admission!*
> *Sending you the love and the light for your highest good!*
> *Faye."*

I took a breath in and pressed "send." I sat still in front of the computer, unable to move, happy and sad, humbled and a little surprised to know that I am still a part of her life, that she came to ask me for help. I smiled; it felt really good.

Suddenly my iPhone made a beep, a notification of an incoming post on Facebook with my name mentioned. I opened it. It was Deanna again. There was a picture of both of us and a dedication: *"This woman is incredible."* As I continued reading her post, I was overcome by the emotion, by her out-pouring of love and gratitude.

> *"She [Faye] taught me that I could take on the world if I wanted to, and I believed her. She taught me how to reach for the stars and never settle for anything less while simultaneously teaching me how to defy gravity. She inspired me to start coaching - to implement in my students what she has ingrained in me. I can only hope and wish that I can influence and inspire my students the same way she has for me."*

I read Deanna's post and felt my energy surging, expanding, and my body becoming lighter. My soul rejoiced as I allowed myself to receive her gift, a gift worth all the years of hard work, sacrifices, tears, laughs, wins, and defeats. She reminded me of the 19-20-year-old girl I once was, filled with dreams of becoming such a teacher that would inspire her students, just like one of my coaches inspired me when I was a little girl. Deanna made me realize that I didn't need to 'become such a teacher,' I already was 'her' and Deanna always saw me like that. Without any awareness, I was the inspiration for her, a role model, just like she is already that for her own students.

Her post made me think of coaches, teachers, mentors, and how they contribute to our lives, how they contributed to mine in particular. Who am I? What were the most important lessons I've learned? How was the meaning in my life defined by them? I reflected upon the ways we touch and shape each other's lives, consciously or unconsciously. And my thoughts took me back in time, when I was a six-year-old skater....

....My mother and my Coach Lana had a long meeting pertaining to me, and my future in skating. I was scared, I didn't expect anything pleasant coming out of this conversation. I knew that Lana hated me and that I get on her nerves. She was a very important coach in my hometown. My mother instructed me to be very respectful, and always do my best, or else, Lana will not teach me. Lana is the best coach *in the whole state of Latvia, and to become a champion, it is absolutely necessary to be coached by her. My mother would do anything for Lana to like me: buy her expensive gifts, escort her to the theater, concerts, take her out to extravagant dinners, or obtain some other inaccessible benefits. And Lana would grind her teeth and coach me, as a favor to my mom.*

She was a petite woman with chestnut-colored long hair, very pretty. Her voice was deep and husky, broken, from constant yelling and smoking. She was single. Her whole life was devoted to her coaching and to her success, regardless of the means she needed to use to accomplish that. She was fast, aggressive, and fiercely competitive. She modeled these qualities to us, her students, and expected us to adopt the same traits. Survival of the fittest reigned among the members of her group. Children were mocking each other, calling names, and even beating, biting, and spitting on each other. This behavior was encouraged by the coaches and the federation as it assisted in developing the specific traits one needed to become a champion. Complaining to grown-ups was prohibited and was a sign of unforgivable weakness. I was quiet, loving, and gentle in nature. I didn't understand why I needed to be fast, aggressive, and competitive. I didn't like what I was experiencing around me and passively refused to follow that lead. As a result, I was an outcast, humiliated daily, called names, etc. My skating skills were stagnating, and no matter how much I was punished, I wasn't getting much better. Finally, it all came down to this meeting between my mother and Lana where she told my mom that it was over. She never saw any potential in me, and I was fat anyway. My mother's eyes were red. She was crying, I could see. She was very upset. I was sad for my mom, but very happy not to see Lana any longer.

My mother, though, couldn't give up on her dream of me becoming a figure skater. She continued taking me to the rink for practice and coached me herself, until one day we were approached by the new teacher: Janna. Contrary to Lana, Janna thought that I was not only incredibly gifted, but had a perfect athletic physique. She singled me out from an ice rink full of little girls. She immediately liked me.

Janna was a quiet, loving, and gentle teacher. She believed in me, and I fell in love with her. I didn't want anything more than to please and be with her forever! I started making rapid progress on the ice, developing impressive skills that very few girls of my age possessed.

Janna moved to my hometown, Riga, from Bashkortostan to attend the prestigious Latvian Institute of Physical Culture. Like the majority of out-of-state students, she lived in the horrible state-owned dorm, where 40 people were sharing one bathroom, and about 15 people were living in the same room. My mother offered Janna to move in with us and have a private room, but in exchange, Janna would train me even when we were at home. I couldn't be happier with the arrangement! My mother didn't need to interfere with my training any longer, and I was in Paradise with Janna by my side. Unfortunately, our work together came abruptly to an end. An excellent student, she got admitted to a highly acclaimed doctorate program in Exercise Physiology in Moscow. She went there to study and do research on energy systems of figure skaters.

Coach Janna invited us to join her, and my mother agreed to go and try out for a couple of weeks. We stayed in a dormitory for elite athletes with three other girls, famous Russian skaters, in the room. I got to skate in Moscow, on the university's ice with famous elite skaters and be one of Janna's research subjects. She used me for her cool experiments, attaching interesting gadgets to my body, having me skate around, and then recording the data. I was fascinated with her studies, fascinated with the laboratory adjacent to the ice rink. When asked who I wanted to be upon growing up, I always thought of her - Janna. As time to go home neared, I felt devastated. I couldn't imagine skating with anybody else. I discovered that it wasn't skating I loved, but Coach Janna. I stopped trying and improving. My mother didn't understand my lack of motivation. She called me 'lazy,' and punished for my sluggishness. I never communicated my feelings to her. I knew that she loved skating, and to earn her approval, I had to do what she said.

Over 30 years went by. People appeared and disappeared on my path; relationships formed and dissolved; lessons taught, learned, and relearned; teachers, disguised in different shapes and forms, presented themselves as missed and acted-upon opportunities. Life was taken for granted and rushed through at times, leaving questions unanswered, and lessons unattended. There was no manual for interpretation and understanding of the events and relationships I encountered. I grew up, and in the course of everyday bustle, I didn't consider the question of how I got to be who I am, what forces were shaping my decisions, desires, drives, values. Deanna's post invited me to open the squeaky door into the past and examine the reasons that inspired or motivated choices I made in my life. I was a student at the University of Santa Monica studying Spiritual Psychology with its laws and principles deeply rooted in acceptance, unconditional loving, self-forgiveness, seeing the loving essence in others, compassion, and gratitude. I realized that both of my coaches, Lana and Janna, greatly contributed to the yearnings of my soul to take up this journey towards becoming a heart-centered coach, and developing the ability of seeing the true essence and potential in others, often hidden behind the mask of fear, anger, spite, avoidance, or laziness.

> *"Some people come in your life as blessings,*
> *others come in your life as lessons."*
> *~Unknown*

As I plunged into my long-forgotten past, I felt sorrow and a deep sense of sadness for a little six-year-old girl who was once me. I felt her confusion and fear of punishment, her anger at the unfairness of life. I sat with her and imagined holding this beautiful little girl in my arms, rocking and comforting her, flooding her with my love. She stopped sobbing, hugged me back tightly, and smiled. A deep sense of peace and gratitude overcame me. I knew she had forgiven herself and others, and together we released all the judgments, and reframed them into blessings. "Incredible!" I thought, "The amazing lesson I was taught by Lana is that violence and anger arises where we are not consciously looking for beauty, love, and higher expression of being, but instead looking for mistakes, wrongs, abnormalities. To grasp this lesson I was served the second half of it in the face of Janna, the direct opposite. She truly saw me as beautiful and immensely talented, and I immediately responded to her vision of me, opening up like a flower."

In the chapter of "Opening Pose" I described my 19-year-old self taking a leap of faith and deciding to attend the University of Delaware, where I could get a degree in coaching figure skating. It wasn't only a 'leap of faith,' it was a moment of inspiration that I experienced during the orientation session. I was shown around the facilities, the rinks, and then biomechanics and exercise physiology lab. Suddenly my inner vision transported me back in time to the University in Moscow:

the rink,

physiology lab,

weird gadgets attached to my body,

my coach,

my childhood role model - Janna...

I immediately knew what I would do next, and what I would do with my life. It would start right here, right now, in this university. I would get this degree in coaching figure skating because I was answering the call of my soul. There was no doubt in my mind that I was making a perfectly right decision. Logically, however, it wasn't only a wrong decision, it was a ridiculous one. I went against tradition, family, and common sense. I didn't follow anyone's advice, suggestions, or wishes. I had no money and had no idea how I was going to pay an out-of-state tuition of $15,000.00 per year. My mother was furious. The Brooklyn College I was attending at a time cost only $600.00 per year and offered the proven professional skill of Accounting. "You are not going any-where!" she yelled. "We will not pay for this school, to be what, a penniless skating coach?!!! You are out of your mind! You never even study, and your grades are barely average. I absolutely cannot justify your momentary whim!" It was true. I never took academics seriously enough to excel in it. My grades were okay, thanks to my good memory and natural intelligence, but I certainly was not an exemplary student. Yet, I knew that this time was going to be different. I would put all my energy and effort into learning all I could to become the best skating coach because that was what I wanted, to emulate Janna. It had meaning to me! Grades, on the other hand, meant nothing at all by themselves, even when accompanied by promises of lucrative job offers down the road.

Twenty-two years later I have to reiterate that I never regretted my decision. I did make the right choice—following the calling of my soul and responding to the inspiration!

Inspiration is a huge driving force behind human achievement. It allows us to move beyond what we deem possible. It transforms us into living gods touching the deepest corners in our hearts. Inspiration doesn't know 'buts', doesn't know doubts, doesn't know fear. It only knows joy and love. When it enters one's life, you have to grab it and follow it. It is a Divine Call. The Universe is dialing you up. Step up to your mission.

———⟨⟨⟨⟩⟩⟩———

When I read Deanna's post again, I suddenly realized that one more of my dreams was on its way to being realized. It was a vision that was born out of meeting a remarkable man, many years ago, during the attendance of my very first Professional Skaters Association's Conference.

I was on the mission to come away with the golden nuggets of invaluable information that would lead me on the path to becoming a coach of many champions. Sure enough, there was a presenter, who had achieved the level of success I was hungry for. He was a gymnastics coach who has produced nine Olympic champions, 15 world champions, 16 European medalists, and six U.S. National Champions, among them such legends as Nadia Comaneci and Mary-Lou Retton. Bela Karolyi was giving his motivational speech at our skating conference. I was sitting in the front row, armed with a notebook and a pen, attempting to catch every word coming out of this ordinary-looking man. Really, there was nothing special in his appearance. He had a slight belly, loosely covered by white polo shirt, and light-colored khakis, not a stylish, dignified presenter by any means. Very soon I realized that it was absolutely impossible for me to take any notes, as with my not-so-good English, and his very heavy Romanian accent, I didn't understand a single word coming out of his mustache-covered mouth. I put my pen down, and began listening to the tone of his voice. It was filled with such enthusiasm and passion that it instantaneously created an atmosphere of uplifting and empowerment. It became clear to me that it was this energy that was the driving force behind the success of his athletes. Even I, a conference attender, felt compelled to jump out of my seat and go to work on my dreams. His voice made me feel like I had grown wings. I immediately enlisted this man as one of my role models. When his speech was finished, the announcer informed us of Karolyi's new book *Feel no Fear* being available for purchase. I went on the mission to get it. Once I got ahold of the book, I literally ate it in one night, armed with a highlighter, a pen, and a notebook. Like a hound, I was on the lookout for the 'secret' behind Bela's out-of-this-world athletic success. I was intrigued by this man, who was never a gymnast or a star athlete himself, an immigrant/refugee, who barely knew any English. What could I learn from him? I was prepared to discover the magic formula. Thereupon, I thought I was inspired by the fact that he trained many Olympic and world champs, and I, too, wanted to accomplish the same feat. But now looking back, I remember a different story that truly inspired me. Before Karolyi became a famous gymnastics coach, he was a newly created PE teacher in a poor rural mining town's grade school. Bela was the first PE teacher this town's children ever had, and they became his first gymnasts. The training and discipline he gave those children transformed their lives, gifting them with confidence, self-worth, and a sense of purpose. He made such an impact on those students that 27 of them became PE teachers. As I read the story, I teared. I imagined myself growing older, being surrounded by my students who are all up-and-coming skating coaches, who I have inspired to step on the path of service, on the path of changing the lives of kids into confident, powerful sources of inspiration themselves. In my mind, this vision represented the ultimate level of success, a legacy, knowing that I truly made a difference in the world. When I read the following line in Deanna's post: "She [Faye] inspired me to start coaching," I felt choked up by the emotion. "She is following in my footsteps! Thank you, the Universe, for letting me experience this joy of knowing that what I was teaching Deanna was meaningful, and the way I taught her was inspiring."

Inspiration. This book couldn't have been written without it.

Inspiration. It is an energy that is more than food and water.

Inspiration. There is so much I wanted to say about it, but instead I feel this lump in my throat and in my heart.

Uninspired, I feel hungry and depressed, yet I know that no amount of chocolate or beautiful things would satisfy this hunger. This chapter was not easy. How could I have written it in a way that not only describes what inspiration was for me, but also would make you leap to your feet and do that which you have always dreamt about but were putting away for a better time? How could I have written it in a way that you, too, would experience this lift, this fire in your heart, light in your head, lightness in your body? I wrote and rewrote this chapter countless times. Inspiration is such a capricious muse! When she enters your life, seize her and follow her! She is a call from the Divine. The Universe is dialing you up. Pick up your call, and follow your muse!

FOOTWORK, STEPS AND TRANSITIONS PRACTICE

• Think of a person or people in your life who inspired you.

• What inspired you about them?

• Would you want to model them? Why? Why is it important to you?

• Are there any specific traits or qualities you notice in them that you admire? You only notice them because you, yourself, have those very same qualities!

• What could you do to cultivate these qualities more?

• Who would you become if you did?

• Now, take a notebook and a pen and write the answers to these questions as fast as you can. Keep your pen moving for at least five minutes. When you are done, notice how you feel. Notice the surge in your energy level. Notice how empowered you feel now. Notice your heartbeat; notice your breathing. Imagine feeling like that every day when you do your work or hobby, spending time with your children or loved ones. Anything! With this energy, you become unstoppable! Keep your notebook with your answers near you every day. Use it! Get into the inspiring, elevated state of energy every day to start living the life of your dreams.

5

Triple Lutz + Triple Loop

Just Imagine...

"If we imagine ourselves as being every bit as huge, deep, mysterious, and awe-inspiring as the night sky, we might begin to appreciate how complicated we are as individuals, and how much of who we are is unknown not only to others but to ourselves."

~ Thomas Moore

5

Triple Lutz+Triple Loop

Just Imagine...

I was on my way to the airport to meet my mom, who was coming for an 'inspection' of our newly bought, old-house, all the way from New York City. As I was mentally preparing for her arrival, I recalled hours of our exchanges on the phone, heated up by her disapproval of our 'immature' decision.

"What are you doing?!!" she would yell into the receiver. "You are buying what? A 42-year-old house?!" I could feel her indignation vibrating through my ear, and I calmly and patiently had to explain to her over and over again that, "No, I don't think we made a mistake." In my many attempts I failed to elucidate to my mom that I had a vision, and I was completely convinced that this **was** 'our' house!

Vision, dream, imagination. Not everyone can buy into it. Often people would get upset and say, "Get real!" But I've learned to trust my own intuition.

I vividly remember the day our realtor took us to see "an old, neglected, outmoded house in a good neighborhood" that we 'might like.' The moment we crossed its crooked, shabby front door, a vision of a little spiritual retreat appeared in my mind's eye! I sat down on the floor and closed my eyes. There I could clearly see my living room furnished in the Asian-inspired Zen style, with sheepskins on the floor and Thai wood-carved panels on the walls. The room felt welcoming, and it instilled the sense of warmth, peace, and tranquility. To my right, the double glass doors led into an elegant but simple office-library filled with our precious book collection. Outside, in the Japanese garden, I could hear the water dripping into the koi pond. My husband, standing in the middle of the room, looked luminous under the sunbeam falling through the imaginary skylights. He, too, was lost in the world of imagination, perhaps, calculations.

"What do you think?" he asked me.

"I think this is it!" I smiled. "I see a house with a great potential, but it needs a lot of work."

"Yeah, I agree. I like it too. Any ideas what we could do with this?" He drew his arms to the side and motioned his head.

"Plenty!" I said excitedly. We signed an offer on the spot, and before long, got sucked into the vortex of ideas and possibilities, challenging our creativity not only in artistic, but also in financial realms.

It was a lengthy and not always pleasant process, with many obstacles and hurdles to overcome. Yet, at last, when we walked into our house for the move-in inspection, we were astonished by the beauty revealed. My Little Spiritual Retreat had manifested!

My mom's plane landed a few minutes early, and she was waiting for me with her bags in the luggage area. Dressed in her favorite velvet burgundy tracksuit, with perfect coiffure and carefully applied lipstick, she smiled and waved at me. I walked over; we hugged, picked up her bags, and loaded them into my car. The whole way home we casually chatted about stuff, both of us completely avoiding the subject of my house. I could definitely feel some tension. She didn't want to show me her anxiety, her worry about my new place of residence she'd never seen, but the horror of which she had imagined. Another turn, and there we were. In the next moment she was walking through the doorway. I, too, felt a little nervous. After all, if she wasn't happy, all of us would experience the storm of her disapproval. As she walked in, I was carefully observing her facial expression. Suddenly, she relaxed, smiled, and all her frown lines magically disappeared. She walked from room to room nodding her head and complimenting everything she laid eyes on. Finally she exclaimed, "I love it! Your house is gorgeous! I would love to have a home just like this one! Is there anything for sale around here?"

"Yes, Mom, there is one. Right across the street from us, the same model home as ours," I replied.

"I am thinking, how wonderful it would be for me to live near you. Can I go tomorrow and check it out?"

"Sure, we can call an agent and ask him to show it to you!"

———⟨∿∿⟩———

As I wrote about the instant my mother changed her mind, the memory of the little girl I once was flowed into my awareness.

I recalled again the time when, as a six-year-old child, I skated in Lana's group and was labeled 'chubby' and 'unpromising,' only because of the appearance of my mom. One look at my short, overweight mom, and Lana knew beyond the shadow of a doubt that a child would turn out as 'defective' as her parent. I received a 'stamp' of disapproval, but at the time, I couldn't understand what was wrong with me. Why couldn't anyone see that I was the most powerful skater in my age group and category? When I looked in the mirror I saw a short, muscular girl whose physique was similar to a very popular-at-that-time Russian pairs skater, Irina Rodnina, a three-time Olympic gold medalist. In my six-year-old mind, I was curious about Irina's stocky shape. How did she become a champion if she was defective like me? Irina was my hero, and I questioned the validity of my coach's preference of skinny, long-legged girls.

Several years ago and some 30 years later, I received an email from a mother of a young skater looking into the lessons with me:

"Dear Miss Faye,

I am writing to inquire about your coaching availability and interest in trying out new skaters..."

We had agreed to meet, and after an initial interview I decided to take her daughter as my student. My mother, visiting me at that time, raised a concern:

"Why did you take her?" she asked me in Russian, motioning her head towards Amanda, my new 10-year-old student. Amanda, overweight, skated past us and did a clumsy under-rotated double jump. Dumbfounded by my mother's question, I wanted to pick an argument. After all these years she was still hypnotized by Lana's obsession and belief that success was only awaiting skinny, long-legged girls. Why couldn't she see past that? While Amanda wasn't in her ideal shape, I was convinced that anyone with desire and discipline could release useless weight, bring themselves into top physical form, and learn the necessary technical skills, required by the demands of the competitive sport. I explained to Amanda and her mother the commitment that would be called for, if they were serious about transforming Amanda into a competitive skater. It was now up to them to decide if they were ready to take their training to the next level, and they said, 'Yes!'

Day after day I watched this girl working relentlessly on improving her skill, hardly ever stopping or complaining. In a short year, she was fit and posting some serious progress. Even peers recognized her as the "Most Improved."

Four years later, Amanda Gelb was smiling off the podium at the 2012 U.S. Nationals in San Jose, while holding her first ever national medal, the bronze. Her road to competitive success was surely not paved with 'rose petals.' While Amanda was rapidly improving, she was falling short of making it out of the Regional competition. Year after year she struggled, but continued to hope and believe that every step she took would bring her closer to her dream.

As I watched the video of Amanda at Nationals, I thought back in time to when I introduced her to 'Stretch Pose' - a very challenging exercise I learned in my yoga class. In it we had to lie on our backs, slightly lifting our feet and shoulders off the floor for as long as we could, while doing a so-called "Breath of Fire." The very first time my teacher demonstrated this asana, he held it for 11 minutes effortlessly! I had a vision! Stretch Pose resembled an air position of a multi-revolution jump, and I saw the benefits it could provide for strengthening a skater's core in a very specific way. To motivate my students to practice this asana, I decided to become their role model. Every morning I would begin with the Stretch Pose, increasing my holding time by a few seconds each practice.

"If you do Stretch Pose every day, and get to hold it for five minutes, you will probably become strong enough to rotate a Double Axel," I suggested to Amanda once. She got excited, and took my advice. Every day we compared our times. I had an advantage of an early start and was always in the lead. When Amanda got her time to about eight or nine minutes, she started training under another coach, and our ways parted.

A few months went by. One day I received a text message from Amanda: "19." I didn't get it. "19 what?" I wanted to write back in response. Then it hit me! Even though Amanda was not working with me any longer, she continued pushing herself on the Stretch Pose! 19 minutes?!!! Wow! Not only is it painful, it is long, so long, like an eternity. It requires getting up 20 minutes earlier in the morning, and then lying on the floor, on the uncomfortable mat in the uncomfortable position, motionless, for 19 minutes!!!! It is a practice of discipline and patience. No one made her do it! That's when I really learned of her unbendable character! This is why Amanda was on that podium in San Jose!

"I saw the angel in the marble
and carved until I set him free."
~Michelangelo

Armed with vision, desire, drive, and unbendable faith, Amanda chiseled her body and mind until she brought her 'angel,' her 'natural' ability, into the light from the depth of her core.

The day following the competition, as she awoke for the first time as a national bronze medalist, she texted her mom:

"Yes!! I told God right before I skated,
that whatever happens I will love him,
and that I will do it to glorify him:-)"

When I shared my writing of Amanda with her mom, Marlene Dunstan, she cried and confirmed that I truthfully reflected the story of her daughter. Marlene then decided to pay it forward by writing a short memoir of a skating mom and her daughter before the most important moment in their competitive life so far. Please, enjoy their journey, as told in her own words by Marlene Dunstan.

Journal – Amanda Gelb
By Marlene Dunstan

*Each of us is born with a "purpose." This purpose was deter-
mined before we were born. Our entire lives are, in essence, a process of
discovering our purpose and then living it out. I once read an insightful
book called,* The Purpose-Driven Life, *by Pastor Rick Warren.
The book was dedicated to me and to you. In the opening, it reads:*

**"Before you were born, God planned this moment in your
life. It is no accident that you are holding this book. God longs for
you to discover the life he created you to live – here on earth, and
forever in Eternity."**

*This is the story of Amanda Gelb, born May 15, 1997, and
her journey in fulfilling her life's purpose. At the young age of two years
old, we were driving down a road on our way home, and we came
across a little red barn with a skating rink. The idea came into my
head that perhaps Amanda might be interested in going skating. I had
always longed to be a figure skater myself, but never had the opportunity
because my parents were too poor. Instead, I spent my years dancing
and performing. So, this was my daughter's chance perhaps, I thought,
just like any parent, always looking for those "missed opportunities"
in their children to fulfill. Amanda responded delightfully, "Yes!" So, I
pulled into the rink, bought two public passes, and rented some skates. I
remember that day like it was yesterday. We had so much fun just edging
our way around the rink, Amanda in between my arms. She loved it so
much that I decided to enroll her in the skating school. From that moment
on, I knew Amanda instinctively was born to be on the ice. She loved it*

so much that oftentimes she would stand at the entrance and cry when it was time to go home. We spent hours upon hours at the rink, even at a young age, because Amanda insisted on staying on the ice. I recall getting her first pair of used skates for $40. Amanda wore those skates all night long in our house with her little teddy bear knee pads. She refused to take them off! So her journey begins...

Twelve years later, and lots of time, money, and sacrifices along the way, we were in San Jose at her first U.S. National Championships. The road to get there was not an easy one for sure. So many long hours at the rinks and long hours on the roads. So many setbacks and injuries incurred. So many frustrations of almost making it past Regionals, and then not making it every year. So many personal struggles internally and externally. As we pulled up to the HP Pavilion for the first time, all those memories rush through my mind, and then I just couldn't believe this was really happening. Amanda had finally made it to Nationals, and I felt actually so humbled inside.

So many years I doubted it would ever be Amanda's turn, but God had different plans, and it just took a lot of patience and faith to get there. Mostly though, it was Amanda's drive and determination to fulfill her purpose. Unlike most of us, Amanda knew her purpose and embraced it from an early age. That is what made her such a driven, hard-working young girl. She was just always doing what she was born to do. She never gave up, but always relentlessly pursued her passion for skating. She also, over the years, developed a strong faith in God and was eager to please Him. When her baby sister passed away a few years ago, Amanda bought a cross at the funeral home with the inscription, "In Christ who gives me strength, I can do all things." This cross she would put in her jacket or gloves before she would compete or take the ice. I realized that Amanda had such an incredible faith, and even when met with failures, she held onto her faith. Countless times I wanted to throw in the towel, but Amanda always had this unwavering confidence it seemed, but it was really her faith that pulled us through to this moment.

When Amanda opened the double doors into the Pavilion, I saw the glow from the bright lights come across her face, and I knew that she had finally arrived at that moment for which God had planned for her all those years. I felt fear and excitement and disbelief all at once! What greater joy than to watch one of your children's dreams become a reality. All I could feel inside was gratitude and humility. Amanda took to the arena ice for the first time for practice, and she just shined, like she was where she was meant to be. Nobody can really prepare themselves for what it will be like to be in a large arena of that magnitude for the first time, and nobody knows how they will react. Although, surprisingly, Amanda did not seem to be any more taken aback by the arena than she was when taking to the ice at home. It just seemed like she was right at home, no matter where she was at!! On the other hand, I was a nervous wreck! I felt anxious and excited and stressed out. Amanda had suffered an injury to her hip only a month before Nationals, and she had to take Advil every day just to be able to train. She also had to cut down her training significantly. Then, she got tendonitis on her left ankle because her boots broke down, and she had to break in new boots with only four weeks to adjust. All the challenges seemed to overwhelm me still, but not Amanda. She was as cool as a cucumber. That's how one of Amanda's coaches always referred to her during competition. But not me, I was not in control, and I was feeling extreme nerves. Amanda would remind me, like she always did when I was stressing out, "Mom, God did not bring me this far to let me go and fail." Again, her amazing faith and reliance on God's promises got us through.

The day of the short competition, Amanda had a really rough practice ice before the official warm-up. Something seemed to frustrate her and she was letting it get to her. She was falling all over the ice. She was angry and seemingly crying. This was a disaster, I thought. Her coaches ran off the ice and with blank stares on their faces asked ME if I knew what to do with her, but I didn't! I was dumbfounded. So, I did what I thought was the right thing, and I took her out to the car so we could talk alone. She explained that she was frustrated because one of her coaches stopped the music after the first jump pass because someone was in her way. She felt that she should just continue on anyway. She allowed her anger and frustration to take over instead of communicating to her coaches what was upsetting her, and she threw the rest of the practice. At this point I reminded Amanda that she was relying on herself instead of God. Sometimes, we have to give up control and remember who is really in control. I told her she needed to let that practice go and to pray. Amanda agreed, and then she took to the warm-up. She skated great and landed all her jumps to her own satisfaction. I was relieved!!

Time for the short program six-minute warm-up at the arena, and it was not going well for Amanda. In fact, she took a really bad fall on a triple Salchow attempt that really shook her. With one minute remaining, she was able to land one double Axel. The warm-up was over and she was the third skater. I was so anxious and nervous, I didn't *know if I could stay and watch. But, I promised Amanda and God that I would stay no matter what. I decided to look up inspirational scriptures on hope, faith, and strength to send to Amanda by texting them to her phone, hoping and praying Amanda would read them and focus on them to help her clear her mind. The moment of truth—the music started and Amanda began her program. She landed a beautiful triple combination; her face lit up, and I knew she was in a good place. She performed an elegant performance and the audience roared! The excitement was overwhelming. Then the scores came up, 43.67!! The high score for her season. Her best score before was 38 points. Everyone was shocked, even her coaches. The short competition ended and Amanda was in second place!! I felt so elated. All I could think of was that I could retire right at that moment or go to Heaven and feel completely satisfied. All the sacrifices were worth it and I could go in peace. I didn't even feel like we needed to do the free skate now. What was the point, I thought. Amanda had already accomplished so much more than I ever dreamed, let's end on a good note. But, Amanda and God had different plans than mine, as always.*

The morning of the free skate, and Amanda had this uncanny peace and confidence about her. The coaches decided that since Amanda had such a difficult practice with them the morning of the short, that they should just let Amanda do her first practice on her own. Amanda had always been at her best when she had the freedom to just be, and every great coach who has mentored her has learned that quality about her. When her mind is free, she just does what she knows. Sure enough, Amanda took to the practice ice all alone, and she was amazing. She landed all her jumps and sections just as she had done them in practice a thousand times! It almost seemed humorous, as her coaches and I sat above in the lounge watching her below do her thing. Some of the greatest coaches of all times were down there with their students, and there Amanda was with herself, and she was brilliant.

The final moment of truth. We arrived at the HP Pavilion an hour before her event was to start, and just the two of us were sitting in the arena together. We had this great "mom and daughter" time to just sit and reflect on everything that brought us to that point. We reflected on all the coaches who had worked with her, Sharon, Barbara, Faye, and how each contributed to the skater she had become. We reflected on some of the greatest "opportunities" or challenges that we had to overcome. I remembered that the ice dancers were competing below and the arena was filled with spectators, but for a moment in time, it felt like just the two of us there. With only five minutes left to spend with Amanda, I wanted to impart some great wisdom or advice to her, but all I could think of was praying. During every difficult or challenging time in my life, praying is all I know and all that I trust in. It is said that when two or more people pray together, that God will hear them, and that if you believe you will receive. So, I took Amanda's hands, in the middle of that large arena, and we prayed together. Then, Amanda's coaches arrived and it was time for her to go down to warm up.

As I waited anxiously, I watched the first group of skaters. All I could think about was whether or not I had the courage to watch when Amanda's group came up. I walked to the top of the arena and sat all by myself. I moved from section to section to see if I could find a comfortable place to watch. But, I was still nervous and anxious! How funny, that my old self who knows better and had prayed earnestly, still refused to relinquish control. I am my own worst enemy. Lots of room for growth still, but I'm getting there. The first group of skaters finished, and I realized that even the highest scores were right in the realm of what Amanda could accomplish. I got more nervous. I saw the next group of skaters come out and there was Amanda. I decided I couldn't watch and I ran out of the arena into the bathroom. I picked a stall at the very end, and I sat on the golden throne in there and prayed. What a sight I must have been! I heard over the loudspeakers that the warm-up had ended and Amanda was the first skater. I heard her music come on and I visualized each element of her program being executed just as she had practiced it. The music ended, and I could barely hear the crowd applauding. I texted everyone to see how she skated, but nobody responded. Ugh! I was so stressed out, not knowing. I walked into the arena and saw Amanda and the coaches on the Jumbotron. I could not read their faces; I had no idea if she skated well or not. My doubt set in, and I thought she did not do well. Then they looked up for the scores. The announcer said 78. . .I was in disbelief! She must have skated well. Another high score for the season. Oh my gosh! Now, I saw everyone's faces light up and everyone was rejoicing. Shame on me, of little faith. Amanda ended in third and she had medaled.

She way exceeded my expectations for her. God had way exceeded my expectations. I felt in shock and humbled once again.

The evening of the awards ceremony was a proud moment. Amanda was finally rewarded for all those years of hard work and dedication. Once again, I thought of all those coaches who had believed in her and had shaped her into the skater she had become. Each one, just as equally important along her journey. They deserved the honor, just as much as Amanda and her current coaching team. I was elated and satisfied. I could hear God in my mind, "Job well done, my child, well done." It was for me and for her. We had followed the path He set forth for us, and this was one of the rewards along the way.

This has been a story of faith, vision, and of purpose. It is not the ending, but just the prelude of things to come for Amanda on her journey. She was once told a story about an old man in a forest and how he just kept going a little farther, a little farther to reach his destiny. I think Amanda is in the forest, just going a little farther on her journey.

This journal is dedicated to Faye Kitariev. She has been a long-time friend to me and coach of Amanda. She has taught me and inspired me along my personal journey. She has also taught and inspired Amanda. To this day, Amanda brings with her all the teachings and disciplines that she was taught by Faye, along with many life lessons and wisdoms. With love and gratitude. . . .Namaste!

After receiving Marlene's letter, I went back and watched the video recording of Amanda's Nationals performance again. Only now I noticed how calm and composed she looked in the beginning of her program, as if she just knew there was no need to worry about anything. Her mission and purpose were strong enough to hold the pressure of the competition under control. After all, didn't she breathe the fire into the core of her being for 19 long minutes per day? Didn't she dream this moment? Didn't she stay committed to her vision? She did!

—∿∿—

In the morning my mother reminded me to make an appointment with the realtor to see the house across the street. I called him in, and he agreed to meet with her later that afternoon. After all the arrangements were agreed upon, I left for work, and my mom stayed in anticipation of a visit to our selling neighbor. When later that day I saw her, she was taken aback and disconcerted.

"Mom, something happened?"

"The neighbor's house, across the street, is terrible! It is an old, outmoded barn!" she exclaimed and shook her head in disappointment.

"Yes, Mom, I know what you mean..." I sighed. She didn't see IT. Her focus concentrated on all the faults and inconveniences a 42-year-old home had, just like other home buyers who had once spurned our house. Yet, the difference between 'outmoded barn' and a living 'paradise,' a chubby little girl and a champion, a beggar and a millionaire, lies in the eye of the beholder, in one's imagination of the unseen potential...

It was then I realized that I had a gift, an <u>ability for seeing beyond the visible</u>. Unconsciously I was using this 'innate faculty' to recognize and tap into my students' "natural" source, even when its existence was not evident to others. I've discovered that we all possess tremendous gifts, some of which we are aware of, and others we don't. <u>We all are the expression of the Divine in the human form</u>, and as such we are all NATURAL! We all have a store of gigantic capability, often dormant, unaccessed, and unutilized. Our "talents" are just small glimpses of what lies within us, like islands in the ocean of potentiality. The "island" may seem isolated, limited, small, and estranged to the islander. But once the 'islander' gathers his courage and ventures out into this 'ocean,' he inevitably discovers more 'lands'. 'He' awakens to the reality of being a part of something greater, and to the possibilities opened by such revelation. <u>It is our birthright to open our eyes and see who we truly are</u> and recognize that all the adepts we know in a class with Mozart, da Vinci, Columbus, Shakespeare, Einstein, Disney, M. Jordan, S. Jobs, and others we may not know as well, are not only us, but also those of us we live with and work with, those we love, and those we hate, those we see as good, and those we see as evil, skinny and fat ones, beautiful and ugly. It takes a paradigm shift from '<u>I'll believe it, when I see it, to believe it, and you'll see it</u>' to recognize the magic all around us, and within us.

> *"Vision is the art of seeing what is invisible to others."*
> *~Jonathan Swift*

My mom didn't live to see the triumph of the overweight, clumsy Amanda... She transitioned six months before that. Like many people my mom was conditioned to see and condemn the 'wrongs,' refusing to even imagine the possibility of a 'change.'

Lana, whom I have met in my adult years, also couldn't see the hidden potential beyond 'imperfect' physical shapes. She was still looking for her skinny, long-legged girls champions, without any success, however. She grew cynical, weary, and disillusioned. It was a surprise for her to see me in great physical shape, so unlike her prediction of me turning into my overweight mom.

It's so easy to write off and reject or allow other people's opinions and expectations dictate the course our lives should take. Yet, the greatest discoveries, music, works of art, athletic achievements, and great innovations were created by rejected visionaries who refused to take 'no' for an answer.

Visionaries who unfailingly BELIEVED that there was more to them than the eye could see.

Visionaries who would walk into an old 'barn' but IMAGINE a 'living paradise.'

Visionaries, who TAKE A RISK and manifest their visions in life.

Visionaries who SEE that there is more to all of us, every single one of us.

Visionaries who KNOW that there is a Sleeping Dragon waiting to be awakened.

> *"Some men see things as they are, and say "Why?"*
> *I dream of things that never were, and say, "Why not?"*
> *~ B. Shaw*

Triple Lutz+Triple Loop Practice

In this exercise I invite you to close your eyes and let your imagination take a flight. Imagine your absolutely perfect life. What do you do, who are you with, where do you live, how do you feel? Allow your creativity to take over. Now, place yourself into this picture. Who are you? How did you change in order to live your ideal life? Once you see the image of your ideal life and your ideal self, write it down in your journal. Be as specific as you can be, and use a lot of descriptive words. Have fun with this process.

6

Triple Flip

"How did you do it?"
"I wanted it!"

"Our deepest fear is not that we are inadequate. Our deepest fear is that we are powerful beyond measure. It is our light, not our darkness that most frightens us. We ask ourselves, 'Who am I to be brilliant, gorgeous, talented, fabulous?' Actually, who are you not to be? You are a child of God. Your playing small does not serve the world. There is nothing enlightened about shrinking so that other people won't feel insecure around you. We are all meant to shine, as children do. We were born to make manifest the glory of God that is within us. It's not just in some of us; it's in everyone. And as we let our own light shine, we unconsciously give other people permission to do the same. As we are liberated from our own fear, our presence automatically liberates others."

~M. Williamson

6

Triple Flip

"How did you do it?"
"I wanted it!"

I am teaching a student a Double Flip. She is not getting it. I am patient with her. After all, it's her first day of attempting a new jump. She appears to be certain in her belief that she cannot land it, and I am not sensing her desire to prove otherwise. She goes for an execution of the jump. I am watching her movements, and I see that even though she seems to be applying all the right techniques, nothing will work, and it doesn't. Not only does she barely get off the ground, but she lands the jump on both feet facing forward, without completing the required rotation. I shake my head, "NO". She comes over and looks at me with expectant eyes.

"Sarah, what did you do with your arms in that Flip?" I ask her. She shows me how her right arm went up, then down, and then in. It looked perfect! She had memorized the movements precisely, but for some reason doing the same thing in the Flip didn't produce the expected result.

"Well, you are doing everything correctly. Why doesn't the jump work for you?" She looks puzzled and shrugs her shoulders. Without going further into the jump technique, I choose to tell her a story instead.

"Imagine a beautiful life-sized model of a car. It looks perfect from the outside, and even inside it looks perfect. What you can't see, is that it has a fake engine. So, the car is not drivable. Why doesn't it have the real engine? Well, the designer was not interested in having this car be driven. He just wanted the shell of the car on display. He just wanted to give people <u>an idea,</u> of what this car will look like, not the actual experience of driving it....<u>You have a great idea about</u> a Double Flip, Sarah!" She listens intently, then smiles as she relates to the car story.

"I know you understand how cars benefit from <u>'real'</u> engines. So, how could your jump benefit from the movements of your arms?"

She nods her head, "My arms could help with the lifting of my body into the air."

"Yes! That's correct! And yet, there must be something else, in order for you to get up into the air and fully rotate the jump. What do you think that might be?" I can see that she is desperately trying to figure out the correct answer, thinking within the frame of the jump technique. Lost in thought, she picks up her water bottle and takes a sip.

"What are you doing?" I ask her. She looks at me apologetically and mumbles, "I am drinking water."

"Why?" I inquire.

She swallows hard and responds in a small voice.

"I was thirsty."

"Aha, so what needed to happen for you to pick up this water bottle and drink out of it?"

Realization starts sinking in:

"I had to want to drink?" She questions her response as it slowly flows into her consciousness.

"Exactly!" I exclaim. "Were you successful in your attempt of drinking water, or did it spill all over the place?"

"I was successful," she replies carefully, pronouncing the words as she is processing the information.

"I see," I say. "Okay, now go do your Double Flip!"

As Sarah skates off, I can see that she is still intently thinking about what just happened. I think to myself, "Now she'll land this Double Flip!" And she does, just like that! She is so excited!

I clap. "How did you do that?"

She smiles and says: "__I wanted it!__"

I wanted it.

I wanted to write this chapter for a while.

I wanted to write a book.

I wanted to teach an Olympic competitor.

I wanted to become a nationally and internationally ranked coach.

I wanted a house, an expensive car, and beautiful jewels.

I wanted luxurious clothing and designer shoes.

I wanted a Chanel bag....

This chapter is about the most magnificent force available to us, humans. It is about the power of 'want.' We use this word hundreds of times per day, but most of the time we don't stop to think about its magic. That's right, MAGIC! Nothing ever happens without 'Want.'

"Miss Faye, you know how you often say that you always get what you want?" my student Angelyn once asked, while offering me a gift bag. I took the bag, and inside I found a book titled *The Secret*. Intrigued, I looked at Angelyn. "This book is about the Law of Attraction, or the law of wanting," she elucidated me. "I saw it in the store and thought about you and about what you are teaching me. I thought you would be interested to know that there is a book written about it, so I got it for you!"

Secret became a huge international success and an eye-opener for many. Yet at the time it came out, I was so consumed by coaching skating that I was unaware of *The Secret's* existence. I literally taught skating during the day, watched skating during the evening, and dreamt skating during the night. If I happened to wander into the bookstore, I immediately went to the sports section, searching for the titles about skating, mental toughness, or a biography of a successful coach. There was no time in my 24 hours to learn about some New Age book. I wasn't even aware of the existence of New Age material, or a self-help section. However, I didn't need to learn about *The Secret*, as it was no 'secret' to me. I have already experienced the Law of Attraction, although I didn't know it was a law. I just happened to notice in the course of my life that if there was something I wanted, I would eventually get it, somehow. *Everything is a result of conception and desire,* was my mantra.

Really, if we take a moment to look around, we would see that every little thing there is was created by someone who wanted to create it for someone who wanted to have it! Here I am speaking about wanting 'things.' Yet, <u>everything around us,</u> everything we use, see, hear, taste, experience is the expression of somebody's will.

As a matter of fact, our life as it is, is really the product of our ambitions. One may say that it doesn't "feel" this way, and yet it is! We are the <u>co-creators</u> of our life! As the name of Esther Hicks' famous book calls it: *Ask, and It Is Given*- it is the law! We <u>ALWAYS</u> get what we want, but often we are either not consciously aware of what it is that we have set our hearts on, or we are not aware of the consequences that accompany the object of desire. So it seems that life is being lived for us, and we didn't get what we have asked for. Or did we?

> *"I can teach anybody how to get what they want out of life.*
> *The problem is that I can't find anybody who can tell*
> *me what they want."*
> ~M. Twain

We begin our journey as innocent children with simple wants and progress into more complex desires.

"I want an ice cream."

"I want a toy."

"I want a cell phone."

"I want a boyfriend."

"I want a husband."

"I want a child."

"I want a house."

We were not concerned with long-term results of our wants. It is later, when we realize that along with the ice cream comes fat on our thighs, broken heart comes with the boyfriend, dealing with somebody else's issues comes with the husband, heartaches and sleepless nights come with the child, outrageous mortgage payments come with the house, a coveted job position comes with the broken family or stress-related sickness. It is later we realize that majority of "wants" brings along the enslavement and disappointment. By that time, however, we have already forgotten that indeed we have received what we wanted, only it came with a certain unplanned-for price.

My client was sitting on the couch in front of me, shaking her head. "I don't know what I want, and I am afraid of wanting.... Well, I wish I could be like you; you are so focused. You know what you want...." I maintained a straight face, listening to her confession, allowing her to fully express her musings. Yet, thinking to myself, "if only she knew what I've been going through..."

Not too long ago I received a questionnaire from my coach, asking me, "What do I want to be like in five years? What kind of life do I want to live? Who do I want to be?

What do I want to accomplish?" Simple questions, but I found myself running from the answers for days. I remembered that I have accomplished what I wanted. I reached the level of success and recognition I wanted. I lived in the house of my dreams. I drove the loaded Infinity and had a closet full of designer clothes. I wanted it all, and I got all of it. I also got things I didn't want; marriage on the brink of divorce, disconnected relationship with my daughter and my family, debts, and colitis. In the beginning of my journey, I had no idea that the destination of my dreams would be so sorry-looking. Obviously, it was NOT what I have wanted. When my coach presented me with these questions, I knew that I had a second chance to 'want' differently. But now I was scared and didn't know what to ask for. What if I got it all 'wrong' again and wasted my precious time to get it 'right'? I am not 20 any longer, and the time to get it 'right' progressively diminishes. I found myself running away from the answers, but the questions were chasing me ever faster.

Another client, and then another one. Faces and bodies change on my couch, but the question remains. A thought crossed my mind, "Maybe this question lives in my office, and it will never leave until I answer it?" It seemed as if the whole Universe conspired and demanded my response.

Suddenly I felt as if I was stuck in the corner and couldn't go anywhere from here. How did I get here? This chapter was meant to be uplifting and inspiring, teach about the magic of wants, show the power we hold in the palms of our hands. But here I was, stuck in the dark corner instead, describing how awful it is to want something. Yet we all see clearly that the progress we made in our civilization was driven by this force....well, the wars were driven by this force as well, and that again was the by-product...I am stuck again!!!!!!!

"What are You trying to tell me?!" I looked up towards Heaven, hoping to hear the answer, searching for the help out of this loop. And it came, or I just imagined that it did; it came from within. Thoughts flowed into my mind, as if from somewhere.

"There is a way to 'want,' and 'get it,' and not have the negative consequences with it," I heard the reply.

"Really? What is this way?"

"Don't you know it already? It's so clear! Your grandest purpose here is to grow and evolve. Satisfying the "wants" for things didn't help you in the evolution of your consciousness. Getting the Chanel bag didn't move you towards the writing of this book; it didn't move you towards deeper inquiries. You have enjoyed receiving it, and I was happy to watch you being excited for a moment, like a child with a new toy. But what then? What are you to do with Chanel bag? My wish for you is to grow spiritually. I give you what you want, and I ask of you to look deeper inside. Do you listen to me? Not usually. You only start searching for me when things are not going as you wanted them to. So we play this game. Now I want you to think, and I want you to feel, feel in your heart, go deeper. All the answers to all your questions are there. I have no doubt you'll find them."

"Well, I have to admit that in the past, I believed that consequences were bad or negative, and I felt sorry for myself and blamed others as a source of my dissatisfaction. As I started seeing upsets as opportunities for growth, things have changed dramatically. Soooo, it is that simple then? We need "wants" as a signpost on the map, to have an idea of direction in which to move. Without it we would be lost, wandering in circles. Then, as Shakespeare put it:

"There is nothing 'good' or 'bad',
but thinketh makes it so!"

Unplanned consequences are neither good, nor bad, but may feel very uncomfortable. They are indicating to us that it's time to grow, shift, and transform."

"Exactly, you've expressed that very well, Faye. Now, I know that there is something else you wanted to speak about in this chapter regarding the 'wants'."

"Yes, that's true! I've noticed how scared and contracted I felt when I thought of the possibility of becoming a teacher of Wayne Dyer's stature and even sharing a stage with him. I was asked to imagine the exact thing I wanted, and it was terrifying. The doubts were creeping in, asking me, "Why do you want that? How will your life change then? Do you deserve it?

I realized then that I've created a box of a certain size that I saw myself fitting into. I realized that I am one of many who <u>are afraid to dream Big,</u> and instead put ourselves in that box. Then <u>we work hard to grow into it, where we should really be working towards growing out of it!</u> The truth is, there is no box outside of our imagination. We become so afraid of disappointments that we stop dreaming, imagining, and going after our dreams."

"This is a very good observation, Faye. But I need to correct you here. You can never stop imagining or creating. You are designed to create. You are creating in your mind continuously. Every thought you think and every emotion you feel carries the creative force within it."

"Does that mean that when we fear disappointments we actually bring them into existence?"

"That's right. That's when you see people 'accomplishing' less than what they are capable of, *growing into the imagined box instead of growing out of the box*' as you cleverly said it earlier. The force of 'I don't want' is just as powerful, if not more powerful, as the force of "I want." The more emotion attached to it, the more capable the thought becomes."

"I think I understand what you are talking about. It comes down to the story of Sarah learning the Double Flip. First, she was afraid of falling on the jump that she thought she wasn't familiar with. As a consequence, she executed an element well below her ability, even though she did all the right movements in the process. But the very next jump she landed, as if by magic. How did she do it? She found the **'why'** that made it important for her to want to land the Double Flip. As this **'why'** crystallized in her mind, the Double Flip became a reality. The jump itself was not nearly as important as her **'why,'** her purpose, the engine behind her **'want'**.

"Yes. This **'why'** needs to be so big and significant to you that every manifested **'want'** will leave you more certain, affirming that you are on the right path, living your life on purpose, with meaning. For this **"why"** you will be willing to go through discomfort of shifts and changes, always learning and growing, keeping Beginner's Mind, open to embrace the possibilities that come, awakening your true potential and sharing it with others."

"Wow, that's it! I got it! Each "want" is like an individual element in the program of the figure skater. The program is the life of purpose and meaning. It is the path that each of us has to fulfill. This purpose is the theme for the program. Everyone is 'skating' a 'program' with a different theme, different storyline that we may or may not be aware of. No 'program' is ever the same. There is a certain amount of joy and satisfaction in completing a "jump" or "spin" successfully. Yet, the 'program' itself is not about an element. It is a mistake to attach yourself to one, once it is completed, and the 'theme' of the 'program' doesn't change depending on how well a Triple Flip was executed."

"Yes. And people around you: all the relationships you have, friendships, co-workers, everybody you touch or meet for a moment or a lifetime, are the audience, the spectators for this program. This program can teach or maybe inspire the audience in big and small ways. It can give them the experience of love and hate, drama and joy, victory and defeat, but ultimately, it can show them their true face of who they are!"

"I love that! You know what I have noticed though, while teaching my students and choreographing their programs? I've noticed that often, they were disconnected from the power of their authentic 'want,' for the sake of satisfying the 'wants' of the teachers or parents, judges or media. So many get lost in trying to figure out how to conform, fit in, and please that they lose their sense of Self, their sense of purpose, passion, and desire. No wonder that they get so disconnected from themselves, feeling hopeless, depressed, unfulfilled, and worst of all, not knowing what they want, or how to want it."

"It is a sad truth in many instances. But you, as a society, condition your young ones from early childhood to want what adults say is 'right' for them, rewarding conformation, and punishing self-expression. People grow up afraid to be different, afraid of being rejected. They would rather sacrifice themselves for the sake of being accepted by their peers, family, community, than excel and own their voice. This is why it is so important to awaken to your purpose and find out what your true 'wants' are. It may be one of the most important questions you may ever ask of yourselves."

"Thank you. I am so grateful to have this dialogue with you, to have this clarity. Thank you, again."

"You are most welcome"

Our conversation stopped. I sat, and kept thinking about it, reflecting, reading and rereading it over and over again, allowing the words to get absorbed into my bloodstream. It all was so new, and yet it felt old at the same time, as if I have always known this. A rush of air beyond my window whisked through the wind bell, creating a beautiful, melodic sound. And all of a sudden I remembered. I remembered a profound little story that had an incredibly powerful effect on me one day.

*It happened one early morning a couple of years ago. There was nothing really special about that morning, and there were no indicators that it was going to be the morning that would alter my view of life. Maybe it was special in a way, that I woke up in a bad mood. As I was getting up, my husband asked me my favorite question: "What do you want?" Immediately I started thinking about the "correct" answer, you know, the one that would make **him** happy. His question put me in a worse mood, than ever before. I chose to ignore him, got up, got dressed, and went outside to the balcony for my daily morning practice of yoga and meditation. As I sat down in meditation, the question of "what do I want" wouldn't leave me alone. I felt stuck and angry and couldn't figure out what it was that I wanted. I thought that I already have everything I wanted. I even thought about my last trip to my favorite mall, when I was walking through the most exclusive, expensive shops, and I didn't want anything! I even called my husband and said, "Honey, there is something wrong with me. I am in South Coast Plaza, and I don't* want anything!" But here I was on the balcony, wrapped in the bright orange-colored wool cape, sitting on my mat layered with a blanket and a purple-colored sheepskin, deep in my contemplation. The early morning darkness was barely dispersed by a flickering light of the tea-light candle, throwing dark shadows on the statue of Gray-Stone Buddha right in front of me. Suddenly, I heard a strange, loud clang. I opened my eyes. There was nothing unusual in my surroundings. I closed my eyes again and tried to concentrate. But as I closed my eyes, a thought crossed my mind that I caught a glimpse of a strange-looking object lying on my mat in front of me. I opened my eyes again, and now I saw it. It was a broken, contorted heavy rubber band. Where did this come from? I was puzzled. On the spur of a moment, I looked up and saw my little gong wind chime hanging from the potted palm tree to my right. A gust of wind moved across it, and the little gong produced a powerful clank I haven't heard before. I took a closer look at this gong, and all at once, I saw it. The clapper was missing a little rubber band which made the sound of the gong softer. Now the raw, exposed wood was hitting against the metal and producing a loud, metallic sound. This was the sound that disturbed my meditation. This sound interrupted my pattern and shifted my attention from what I want, to what does the little gong want. And I got it! The little gong wanted to be heard! It couldn't be heard before since the rubber band was hushing its voice. The little gong snapped its constricting, voice-stopping rubber band, and now it could stand strong on its own, and dong loudly its truth. And just like that, I knew that I, too, like my courageous little gong wind chime, want to be heard. I too get mad when my words get stuck in my throat and I am unable to speak, to express myself, to stand up full in the truth and beauty of who I am.

*In that moment I knew why I am doing what I am doing. I want to be heard. I want to make a difference in people's lives. I was inspired by the strength and beauty of the little innocent gong. It snapped a half-inch thick rubber band to be heard! What can I, a Human, do then? What can you? Where is your voice? How do you speak? How do you express yourself, through which medium? You are an athlete, a dancer, a singer, an artist, a writer, an actor, a coach, a parent, a person. Are you being heard? What do **you** need to do to snap **your** rubber band?*

TRIPLE FLIP PRACTICE

To assist with discovery of your inner wants, I encourage you to read through the paragraph below, then if you wish, follow through with the exercise.

Please find a comfortable, quiet place, where you wouldn't be disturbed. Close your eyes and breathe in deeply into your belly. As you exhale, let go of all the worries and concerns. Allow yourself to completely relax. Once in the relaxed state, ask yourself: "What do I really want to experience in my life? What would make me feel happy, vibrant, alive? What does make me feel happy, vibrant, alive now?" Notice what thoughts come into your awareness, vision, feelings? Open your eyes, pick up a pen and your journal, and write down whatever it was that came forward for you. If nothing came forward, hold on to your questions as you go through your day/days. The answer may appear unexpectedly anywhere—in a book, movie, TV show, friend's remark. Notice what makes your heart 'sing.'

7

Triple Flip + Triple Toe

The Magic of Decision

"Sir, what is the secret of your success?"
a reporter asked a bank president.
"Two words."
"And, sir, what are they?"
"Good decisions."
"And how do you make good decisions?"
"One word."
"And sir, what is that?"
"Experience."
"And how do you get Experience?"
"Two words."

"And, sir, what are they?"
"Bad decisions."

~Unknown author

7

Triple Flip + Triple Toe

The Magic of Decision

I am surrounded by thousands of people. It is midnight, and there is a sea of barefoot folks marching the streets of downtown Los Angeles. I am one of them. I am excited and scared at the same time. I don't exactly know what to expect. One thing is for certain; I first want to see how other people will do it, and then, somehow, I'll know I can do it too. I made up my mind. There is no way I am turning back now. I am surrounded, and the current of moving bodies now almost carries me over. We are coming closer to our destination, and I hear the hypnotic beat of tribal-sounding drums. I am trying to get through the people to come closer to see the action. I hear Him speak, motivating people, encouraging them, inspiring. My heart tunes in to the drumming, and starts beating faster. All of a sudden there is no one in front of me, and two men by my side order: "Walk!" What?!!! NOW?!!! I am not ready yet!!!! I feel the urgency from the crowd behind me. I have two choices—to step out and forget about the whole thing, or walk. In front of me is a several-feet-long grass lawn with the glowing red hot coals, looking at me, testing my strength of heart. There is no turning back. Decision is made. I have committed. Okay! I take a deep, long breath in, look up and in front of me, and make a move. "Cool Moss. Cool Moss, Cool Moss," I almost chant in tune with the drums as I march in cadence over the coals. Next thing, I hear screaming and people jumping on me, hugging and congratulating. I barely noticed what happened. It went so fast. Surprised I didn't feel any pain. Now, as I slowly walk back by myself into the convention hall, the thought of what just happened creeped into my mind. "I AM A FIREWALKER!" I don't know yet what it will mean in my life. But I know with certainty now that I AM A FIREWALKER!

"You look so good," complimented my classmate. "How do you do it?"

"I only eat raw vegan food," I replied.

"Wow! And how is your relationship?" It was odd that he asked this question next, yet in the precise moment the timing felt perfect, as if I was expecting his question. I had been working on myself; my diet, my relationship, my attitudes, and my habits. I had accepted his inquiry as a feedback that the efforts I put forth into working with myself had begun sprouting. I was preparing to kick off in my new career—coaching people on the principles of awakening to their inner potential. I wanted to inspire my prospects to change and grow. To do that, I believed I had to transform myself first: improve my health and appearance, and my relationship. The leaders I followed walked the talk and so I embodied the principles I was about to use to coach others.

"Amazing!" I heard myself almost singing the answer and experiencing my whole body filling up with joy. He nodded his head, and the look on his face was saying, "Just like I thought. Maybe I can have that one day also..."

He was overweight and insecure, trapped in a relationship that was not giving him fulfillment. He even looked shorter under the weight of all his problems. We were standing outside the parking garage late into the evening, talking after the class. I got to facilitate him earlier that evening and struck the sensitive issue that he wanted to resolve. He seemed desperately wanting to make changes in his life, and he looked at me, hopeful that I could help him. I saw how invested he was in his problems, how they clouded his view. Problems have a tendency to do that. They are like a heavy gray fog up in the mountains that obscures your view of the road and freeze you, making the drive difficult and scary. I knew that he was clinging to his food as a way of shielding himself from pain, looking for comfort. But it never lasted very long. Guilt and disgust always follow the indulgence with food. He wanted to break free from the trap but was afraid to make changes. His problems were familiar to him and provided a level of certainty, like a chronic ache that one is so used to and learns to ignore.

"Habit is either the best of servants,
or the worst of masters"
~N. Emmons

I searched for words to empower him to take control of his life the way he wanted. I observed the struggle between two aspects of him, one that was eager to break free, and the other one that preferred to keep things as they were.

It occurred to me that only a few short months before, I was 15 pounds overweight and struggling in my relationship, not because of my weight, but more of the neglect and avoidance. Then I signed up and attended Tony Robbins' event to get a little jump start and inspiration for writing this book. As Tony talked, I started seeing more clearly what I wanted to do with the next phase of my life and who I would have to become in order to do that.

I watched Tony presenting from the stage some feet away. He was moving with passion and energy, fire coming out of his eyes, and I felt something shift inside of me. Robbins, at 52, looked and moved like a 20-year-old athlete! His body was lean and supple. I just imagined having the energy that Tony had! What could I do with that energy? What could I not do? In that moment, I decided that I will do what it takes to attain it!

"Once you make a decision, the universe
conspires to make it happen."
~ Ralph Waldo Emerson

I came home that night, dancing around my living room. My family collectively decided that I was crazy. It was my birthday, and I attributed my uplifted attitude to that. They really didn't need to know what kind of experience I had, what I decided to do, and why. But the very next day I started moving in a new direction. I made a decision to reinvent myself again: lose weight, improve my relationship with my husband and daughter, change my diet. I had decided to become a role model and an inspiration to others. And now I had an opportunity to empower and inspire this person in front of me.

"Imagine you are in Paris, and you don't have a map," I said. "You want to go see the Eiffel Tower. How can you find it? Where would you choose to look, at your feet, or up?"

"Up, of course," he replied.

"That's right. You would keep your eyes fixed on your target until you would get to your destination. Here is the same thing. You want to see the Eiffel Tower; look up, keep your eyes focused on it, and move your feet. Rick Godwin once said it perfectly:

> *"One reason people resist change is that they focus on what they have to GIVE UP, rather than what they have to GAIN!"*

"Yes, exactly! I understand." He smiled.

As I talked to my classmate who was standing in the crossroads of his life, overweight and unsure of his next move, I felt the power and desire within me to guide him, to guide others like him, on the path of harnessing the power we hold in our hands called Life. Yes, change is uncomfortable. He wanted to release excess weight, begin an exercise program, and eat healthy, but had difficulty letting go of old habits.

"You know, I firewalked." I just threw that one in.

His eyes got big and wide.

"You did?!! Did it hurt? Were you scared?"

"I was scared, yes. But it didn't hurt. AT ALL! Do you want to know how I did that?"

"Yes, of course!"

"**I made a DECISION.** I just made a simple DECISION to walk, and off I went, without looking back, of course. There was no looking back, or putting one foot into the fire, and leaving the other foot on the grass while thinking, *to walk or not.* **You decide, and either you walk or you don't!** You can't be in-between. In-between is where you burn. It doesn't hurt to walk, but it would be very painful to stay and linger in the indecision."

"That's it? It is so simple. I have to make a decision!" He looked like a happy child who had found his long lost favorite toy. I smiled at him.

I remembered how energizing it feels, once the decision is made!

I remembered the feeling of freedom, as if the sea got parted and you can just move freely.

I remembered how it is tremendously empowering to MAKE A DECISION and begin the journey of realizing what you want!

"You don't have to see the whole staircase, just take the first step."
~Dr. M. L. King, Jr.

Yet, we are often afraid to make that first step. How often we wished that someone else made it for us?!

"If change is what you truly want," I told him, "make a decision and step forward with it! Be truthful in your intentions! Making a decision doesn't have to mean that you close the door on the past forever, but it will give you clarity and energy to move in the new direction.....Think about what you will have to endure if you don't make that decision. How much longer are you willing to suffer? How much longer are you willing to make others around you suffer as a result?" I gave him a few moments to think about it.

"It's getting late. I think we need to go now. Tomorrow is a long day," I said. He agreed, got his garage-opening card out of the jeans pocket, and opened the door for me. We both disappeared in the darkened parking structure, dimly lit by the emergency lights. All the students from our class were gone by now. We dipped into the silence, only disturbed by the echoing sounds of our steps.

"Do you need a lift to your car?" My words echoed in the empty building.

"Yes, please." He nodded.

We got into my car, and I started the engine.

"You know, I talk too much. But I have to confess, helping you today gave me an opportunity to practice 'coaching', and I want to thank you for that." I looked at him, and he smiled back gratefully. "Would you be so kind as to tell me what was most helpful for you in our conversation?"

"The part about making a DECISION. Definitely, it was most helpful!"

I felt so light and happy to assist someone, even in a small way. It energized and empowered me!

It was a little past midnight, but I wasn't sleepy at all. I entered my hotel room, sat on my bed, and just reflected in silence upon the conversation I just had. As I closed my eyes, I saw myself walking back to the LA Convention Center after the firewalk.

I look around, and there is a little old man with a walking stick, walking proudly a few steps behind me. He, too, is a Firewalker, and many daredevils behind us, and in front of us also. All of a sudden I recognize that my classmate, too, is a Firewalker. He could be, if he made that choice and had the opportunity. I know that every time anyone makes a decision to push themselves to go further to the place they have not been before, while being scared, insecure, vulnerable, but take that step anyway, against all odds and common sense, they, too, become: The FIREWALKERS! It is in our blood to push ourselves to the limits of our imagination. That's it! The limits of our imagination. And one can look at me puzzled, "Imagination doesn't have limits," he might say, and I will answer back, "You're right, and so you, too, have no limits."

I pulled out my daily journal and wrote: "Next chapter for my book will be about making a DECISION."

TRIPLE FLIP+TRIPLE TOE PRACTICE

You've connected with your purpose, discovered inspiration, imagined possibilities, and defined what you truly want. Now is the time to move forward or retreat. It's the time of decision! It's the time to decide to go for it and take an action, or choose to go back and stay where you were. This is a breakthrough moment. Our power lies in the moment of decision. So, what are **you** going to decide?

8

Triple Lutz

I Know I Can!

One day a human went to Heaven in the way that humans do. Upon arrival, the human was greeted by a host of angels and given a tour of all of Heaven's wonders. Over the course of the tour, the human noticed that there was one room the angels quickly glided past each time they approached it.

"What's in that room?" the human asked?

The angels looked at each other as if they've been dreading the question. Finally, one of them stepped forward and said kindly, "We're not allowed to keep you out, but please believe us—you don't want to go in there!"

The human's mind raced at the thought of what might be contained in that room. What could be so horrible that all the angels of Heaven would want to hide it away? The human knew that one should probably take angels at their word, but found it very hard to resist temptation. "After all," the human thought, "I'm only human."

Slowly walking toward the room, the human was filled with dread and wonder about what horrors might be about to be revealed. But in fact, the room was filled with the most wonderful things imaginable: a beautiful home, nice things, great wisdom, a happy family, loving friends, and riches beyond measure.

Eyes wide, the human turned back to the angels. "But why didn't you want me to come in here? This room is filled with the most amazing things I've ever seen."

The angels looked back at each other sadly, then back at the human.

"These were all the things you were meant to have while you were on Earth, but you never believed you could have them."

~Unknown

8

Triple Lutz

I Know I Can!

Yesterday was a special day. It would have been my mother's 64th birthday, and I got to sit down and remember all the great gifts I have received from her and my dad, gifts I had not appreciated before.

My parents were not my heroes when I was growing up. I didn't understand them. I was too self-absorbed to contemplate who they were, other than food and shelter providers, and 'taskmasters'. I took them for granted, as most children do. After all, in my world, all children arrived with some sort of parents, some better than others. I never thought about what kind of world my parents lived in, how they felt, or what beliefs they held. I was mainly concerned with my own well-being, and as such, I held a lot of upset feelings against my mom. I perceived her as harsh, straightforward, and often mean. She had a very short temper and had difficulty containing her volcanic nature within. As a result I would often experience her heavy hand, the dancing of a thin leather belt on my body, or sharp, painful words, indicating that I didn't do as well as she expected. I grew up terrified of awakening the impatient beast within her.

When she was 40 years old, a shift in the political situation in the Soviet Union presented my parents with a long-sought-after opportunity—to immigrate to the United States. Without much hesitation they quickly decided to act upon it and filed the necessary documents requesting our release from the USSR. Once the exit permit was granted, the preparations for our departure began.

For 10 years my mother had dreamed of this moment: going to America, seeing her brother, having access to fashionable clothes, delicious food, and all the amenities of comfortable living available to people in other countries. But now it was real, no longer a dream. She could finally realize what she wanted for so long. Suddenly, everything became crystal clear to her. She agreed to 'jumping off the cliff' with two children and a husband and flying into the realms of an unknown foreign land—with unfamiliar rules and a language neither one of us could speak. She had no 'real' professional training to lean on for support. In the USSR she was able to find her way around living by her wit, savviness, and creativity, finding opportunities invisible to others. She developed a gift of intuiting how to win over the higher-ups and make important friends. While she was proud of her abilities, she considered herself an undeserving impostor for the lack of higher education. These feelings were a source of tremendous stress and fear that her 'skills' would be useless in America, where people were 'honestly' earning their incomes. She also couldn't bring herself to trust my dad's ability to provide for the family. She had little respect for his prowess as a musician – a drummer, to earn a sustainable livelihood.

My dad, on the other hand, never wanted to emigrate, until that moment. He was very devoted to his band and his music. But all of a sudden, he became very enthusiastic and inspired by the proposition of a fresh start. The dangers of being lost in an unknown country didn't seem to scare him. Every morning he would wake up renewed, energized, with a sense of purpose and knowing. He put his headphones on, Walkman on his belt with the English tapes playing continuously, and ran errands in preparation for our departure. He seemed oblivious to the enormity of his sacrifice: music, his mother, all the relatives, house, friends, language, job with secure earnings, and ultimately, his identity. Many had questioned my parents' judgment. Why did they choose to leave the familiarity and security of their lives and go far away, where you have no idea what will happen of you and your family? My dad told me that he wanted me and my sister to have a better life. Perhaps he could see that there was no future for us, his daughters, in the Soviet Union. I was young and never questioned the sanity of my parents' will, what they went through, and what their experience was like emotionally, physically, mentally, and spiritually. Something within them dictated that it was the right thing to do, that there was more to them and our lives than what we had under present conditions.

My father possessed a rare gift. He could put the 'blinders' on and stay focused on the goal in front of him, never being sidetracked by anything. He didn't look back and carried no regrets. He appeared confident in what he had—his head and his heart—and was prepared to put them both to work, finding his way in the Land of Opportunities. He annoyed me tremendously by his constant nagging and lecturing to sit and study English when all I wanted to do was to hang out with friends and go window shopping.

I close my eyes and can vividly see an image of my dad: his neatly cut beard and mustache, kind brown eyes, thick wavy black hair touched by silver and fashionably styled, dressed in a colorful sweater over a dress shirt, beige slacks, and a customary Walkman on the belt completing his attire. He is droning on, reciting English phrases while packing boxes of stuff in our little apartment in our hometown of Riga, selling traditional Russian wooden dolls, Matryoushkas, on the streets of our transitory destination point, Rome, or cleaning offices in a new hometown, Brooklyn. In my mind's eye, everything he's doing is slow with meticulous attention to detail.

He came to 'discover America,' but now I understand that he really came to America to discover himself. He surrendered his 'musician's' identity and adopted a 'beginner's mind', open for an opportunity to learn a new trade, yet having no idea which way to go. He simply believed that if he moved his feet one step at a time, success would follow.

His long-time friend, a major insurance broker in New York, became fascinated with my dad's dedication to excellence. He speculated that my dad possessed just the right traits to become an accomplished insurance agent and convinced him to give it a shot. The 'ball' landed by my dad's feet, and he enthusiastically picked it up. His friend warned him of the intense studying required to receive the broker's license, loaned him several thick books, and suggested he study them thoroughly. My dad didn't mind. Earphones on, every morning he marched off to the office where he held a 'cleaning warrior's' position, and while cutting through the mess, and slaying the dirt, he was making improvements in English proficiency. By night, armed with patience and enormous dictionaries, he was deciphering the 'coded' legal language of insurance. In six months a newly licensed broker, Valery Kovler, my dad, convinced his first client to cover his life. Three years later our entire family traveled to a huge convention held in Beverly Hills, where my dad was presented with his first award as a national leader in the insurance industry.

My mother's path was not filled with disciplined commitment and dedicated learning. She was a complete opposite of my dad. Her quick temperament didn't allow for diligent and patient acquisition of new skills, and instead searched for opportunities where she could apply her wit, intuition, and charm. She thought herself 'lucky' to find just the job she was perfectly suited for: an admissions counselor in the trade school for Russian immigrants. It wasn't just a job for her; she identified herself with the success of the school. She could easily intuit what needed to be said or done, connecting with the clients and understanding her boss. Passionately convinced, she talked to prospective students. They listened to her and enrolled one after another. The school grew, and my mother got a position of an admissions director. Work was always on her mind, and she talked about it all the time. She regarded her school so highly that people thought she was speaking about some major university! I would often get irritated with her and her advice. I was a strong advocate for a formal education, and judged my mother as narrow-minded and confused.

When holidays came about, she received tokens of appreciation in abundance: Her office would get flooded with flowers, chocolates, and small gifts. People flocked to her for advice and inspiration and were grateful for her help. She desperately wanted my approval. She wanted me to care about her accomplishments, wanted me to be proud of her, but I, consumed by my own successes, was insensitive. Like many children, I neither cared about the work she did, nor about the love and appreciation she was receiving from her co-workers, boss, and students. Misunderstood, I perceived her as a selfish bragger...

Weeks after my mom's transition, I received a phone call. It was Anya, her young colleague and protege. In tears Anya told me about the impact my mother had on her life. "Gita was my lantern, my guide. She helped me to find myself. She was like a mother to me, closer than my own mom. I feel so lost. What will I do now without her? Who will guide me?" her voice was shaking as she was fighting back her tears.

Anya came to the U.S. from a small provincial town in Russia all by herself. She left her family behind and now felt lonely and lost in the humongous, fast-paced life of New York City. She was barely 19 or 20 years old. My mother took Anya under her wing, gave her a job, trained her, and offered a place to stay. Anya, in gratitude, gifted my mom with the kind of love neither I nor my sister were willing to give. Anya was the person who spent the most time with my mother during the last few months of her life. "Faen'ka, I can't imagine being in the office without Gita being there. She held up the whole school with her exuberance. Everyone was going to her for help. Your mom was such an inspiration!" As we continued talking, I felt as if Anya was my misplaced baby sister, and it was my responsibility to step into my mother's shoes to comfort her and provide direction. She was so thankful for my help. I smiled, knowing that my mom would have been happy that I helped her Anya.

When I hung up the phone, I sat on my bed in my bedroom, looking into the mirror, into my own eyes. Dark brown eyes were staring back at me from the reflection, so much like my mom's. Suddenly I realized what my mother did in her life. She was a life coach, who had empowered and inspired thousands of feeling-lost immigrants to believe in themselves to build a new life in the U.S. As her eyes looked back at me from the mirror, I knew with absolute certainty that I, too, possess the same gift and passion for inspiring people to discover their 'new' lives filled with meaning, and their 'new' identities, their authentic selves. Ironically, my mom's cubicle displayed a number of photos depicting me and my students, as she shared with her clients my achievements in the world of competitive figure skating. She used my example to inspire them to believe in themselves, to believe that anything is possible! As I looked into those eyes in the mirror, they filled with tears of gratitude and appreciation: I finally knew who my mother was; I knew who my dad was. I recognized them; they were Dragons. It's just that I couldn't see it while my Dragon was sleeping. Perhaps, I wasn't ready then. Now, I was astonished to discover that my power of believing in myself I inherited from two remarkable people, my parents, who believed that nothing was impossible. I sat on the bed and cried, cried for all the times I didn't get my parents, cried for a lost opportunity to tell them that I appreciated and loved them, cried for all their advice I didn't hear because I knew better, and cried for all the questions I had for them that will never be answered. I cried and made a decision to leave skating behind and take up a leadership position. For I, too, like my mom, can passionately inspire people to follow their dreams and develop their potentials, and like my dad, devote my life to learning and growing one small step at a time. I cried more, but I didn't feel sad anymore. I now felt happy, as if I had found a part of myself that had been lost. I felt as if I finally understood what my destiny is all about. I was an extension of my parents' lives, and it was up to me to take it to the next level.

I called my aunt to share revelations about my parents, but in the process of casual "how-are-yous" the conversation took a different direction.

"I hear you are getting a Master's Degree in psychology? What are you planning to do with it?" she asked.

"I am thinking of performance coaching," I replied.

"What does that mean? What are you going to do?"

I carefully explained to her about the calling I have: to assist people in finding their life's purpose, realizing their potential, and empowering them to follow their dreams. She listened, and then dismissed me: "All people have their limits. Some have special talents and can go further; others can only go so far, and no one can change that." I felt an urge to argue, prove that she was wrong, and I was right, but I changed my mind. People hold certain beliefs, and these beliefs shape their lives.

"What you believe is essential to the quality of your everyday life experience. The reason why this is so important is because people's lives unfold in accordance with what they believe to be true!"
~Ron and Mary Hulnick, Ph.D.

I thought of my friend, an Israeli ice dancer, Galit Chait. She was a chubby, cute 'wanna-be' young skater, an average athlete with no particular talent. She was, however, a diligent student, and since her parents were also willing to financially support her lessons, she was receiving them in abundance. Her body, despite all the efforts, was awkward in movement, and her competitive records were reflecting this fact. Despite the collective opinion by the skating community that she'd reached the limit of her potential, she secretly believed that she would become an elite, world-class skater.

When Galit was in her teens, her dad took her to Russia during one of his business trips. One of the coaches there suggested she try ice dancing. The coach called Max, a retired skater, a former Junior World silver medalist, and asked him to skate with Galit.

"Let her experience what ice dancing is all about."

As the two of them skated, holding hands, a young teenage girl fell in love. The dreams of competing together, sharing the ice, and training with another soul danced in her head.

I remember meeting her around that time, when she first appeared at the University of Delaware's Ice Training Center with her 'exported' Russian dance partner.

I was a student at the university, earning a degree in coaching figure skating. When my classes were done for a day, I worked as an off-ice conditioning program facilitator. The gym, where I worked, was strategically located above the main ice surface. Every day I had a chance to watch training sessions: dance and pairs, and then design weightlifting programs for those skaters to improve their performance. That day I was sitting on a stool by the balustrade prepared to watch another session when a new couple took a freshly cut ice. Young guy in his early 20s; tall, beautiful, confident skater; and a teenage girl, a cute, petite blonde, little shy. I didn't know their names, but I was certain that both of them would be introduced to me soon, as they would come to the weight room for sure.

The new couple skated their program, a "Pink Panther". It was interesting and unique, and I admired the composition. It was cleverly choreographed, masking the girl's weaknesses and emphasizing the guy's strengths.

Later we became very close friends, and of course, we got to know each other better. Galit shared an apartment with her partner, and I was always admiring how neat, clean, and organized it was. Every little thing had its place, and she wouldn't retire for the night until everything was in order. Delaware was a place where many out-of-town skaters trained, and, like Galit, lived without their parents. They skated by day and partied by night. While everyone was partying, Galit led a quiet, focused life. I highly regarded her character: perseverance, focus, determination, unbelievable work ethics, unbending discipline, and a huge sense of responsibility. Her parents were backing her up, and she could have anything she wanted. But she was very respectful to the money she received from them and lived a modest life. This was a 17-year-old girl! I was four years older than she, yet I looked up to her as my role model. She knew what she wanted and worked hard towards her goals. Some people would quietly laugh at Galit behind her back, judging her as naive and weird. After all, she had no talent, lacked flow and flexibility, and frankly, wasn't going anywhere, no matter how hard she tried. Galit and Max got sixth at Nationals and weren't likely to move any higher than that anytime soon.

But something else happened. A window of opportunity opened, and Galit, Israeli-born, could represent Israel at international competitions. Finally, her dream of becoming a World competitor materialized. I now impatiently waited for the results from the Worlds as I had from the Nationals. In her first World Championship she finished in distant 28th place. Some people ironically smiled: "What did she think she was going to get?" But Galit didn't care. She was there now, focused, working hard, committed more than ever.

Her relationship with Max deteriorated. She was demanding more and more work. He was tired. He couldn't keep up with this girl who was falling down exhausted, crying from unbearable fatigue, but still getting up and stubbornly going forward. A change needed to take place for Galit to move towards her dreams. She split with Max, and a new partner knocked on her door, Sergei. He, too, was devoted and hungry. He could see the fire behind Galit's eyes, fire that was shining so strong that it eclipsed her skill deficiency. He recognized that with the kind of belief and desire she held, they could move mountains, and that's what he was looking for in his partner. When in 2002, their seventh World Championship together, they won a bronze medal, my heart leaped in joy! "She did it!

She did it! She did it!" I screamed and jumped up and down repeatedly.

"Did what? Who did it?" The nanny of my baby daughter ran into the family room where I was glued to the TV screen.

"My friend Galit, she just won her first World medal!" I almost screamed I was so excited.

"I see," she calmly smiled, indicating that perhaps I was a little overreacting screaming like this.

"You just don't understand. She is not conventionally 'talented,' but she believed she could do it. She worked so hard to prove it to herself, prove it to the world, and here she is: a living testimony that the impossible is possible! If she could do it, anyone can, if they truly want it. I know I can! It's not in some of us, it's in all of us! Not everyone is willing to go that far, so they create this belief for themselves of what they can and cannot achieve. The truth is: <u>There are no limits in human potential, there are limits in human beliefs!</u>"

TRIPLE LUTZ PRACTICE

I hear that before you can begin moving forward, certain conditions must be fulfilled, stars align, and barriers overcome. Whatever it is, I'd like you to ask yourself these simple questions: "Is it true? Am I absolutely sure? Whose voice is telling me that I can't right now? Is it my mom's, my first grade teacher's, or my boss? Is it still true today? Can I update my belief into something that I know is truer?" Write down the new belief. Walk around with it, repeating it to yourself. How does that sound? If you feel more freedom, lightness, and excitement, congratulations! You found a new belief that serves you.

9

Double Axel+Double Toe+Double Loop

Flashlight in the Darkness

"What lies behind us and what lies before us
are tiny matters compared to what lies within us."

~O. W. Holmes Sr.

9

Double Axel + Double
Toe + Double Loop

Flashlight in the Darkness

I was sitting on the bench one day by the entrance to the ice, carefully observing my student. She was gathering the speed, skating in preparation of launching into the twirl of a double Salchow. She had learned to execute this jump perfectly some time ago. She jumped, revolved, and nailed the landing with seemingly little effort, and a great precision. Yet all of a sudden, I notice the constricting feeling of anger settling in my chest, making it difficult to breathe. I noticed that I was angry with her execution of the jump. I also felt hopeless and bored.

Somehow, I KNEW that what she did was terribly wrong. She came back to me for feedback, and I struggled to find the words to explain my disappointment to a 10-year-old girl who was happy with the outcome of her efforts. But at that moment all I could feel was that I'd been cheated. Cheated like a spectator who was promised a captivating show by a world-famous performer, but instead received an average show by a filling-in amateur. I struggled to keep my composure and relate the feedback calmly:

"Sarah, I saw an excellent double Salchow with my eyes, but....with my heart I saw NOTHING!!!!!"

As I was talking to her, I felt the feeling of frustration rising ever higher. I heard myself repeating this empty word "nothing" over and over again.

"What is the point of going through the mechanics of a well-known element without any feeling, Sarah?"

The words echoed in my mind, taking me back in time to when reaching deep within to feel the movement inside out became my obsession.

It was July of 2007, and three-time U.S. National Champion Johnny Weir asked me to choreograph his short program.

There was something magical about Johnny's way of skating. It was not about the elements. It was not even evident right away what it was that made his skating so special. It's just that it made you feel good, happy, light. It brought the goosebumps. I had never experienced THAT with any skater before. I'd taught great skating. My students were awesome athletes and were regarded as some of the best in our region, even nation at their respective levels. I was happy with our results. But that day, when Johnny came to skate with me, I saw, my "great" skaters, national competitors, pale in comparison as if they were beginners. But it's not even fair to say that. Johnny appeared as if he was a different breed altogether. He was ALIVE, while my skaters were beautifully molded, empty Barbie dolls.

Now I understand that my skaters were awesome when one saw them with their eyes. But Johnny's skating commanded watching with one's heart. He was the skating himself, the spirit of loving energy transmitted through the skates into the ice and into the hearts of the spectators, even when he didn't seem to be doing any significantly difficult elements. I don't even know if he realized that, if it was in his conscious effort. People were recognizing Johnny as "gifted" and his skating as "Natural." They called him "Natural", because it seemed that everything he did came with such ease, grace, and lightness. They also called him an Artist. No one could seemingly put a finger on what it was that they were drawn to so much.

His skating awoke my heart and opened the wound of longing, longing to experience this loving energy again, energy that I forgotten many years ago, as a 16-year-old girl falling in love for the first time, when I believed that anything was possible.

When our program was choreographed, Johnny was gone out of my life, like a summer breeze. He left me with the realization of emptiness in my heart and the knowing that there was a way to fill this emptiness up, that this energy didn't only exist in Johnny, but it was within me and you and the Universe, and I just needed to find a door *and a key to access it, to connect with it. Through the stroke of "luck" or "coincidences" or "synchronicities", I saw musicians, dancers, and martial artists who had access to the same field of energy as Johnny. It reassured me that there was nothing "magical" or "super special" about Johnny other than he knew how to access this field that is invisible to most. Yes, he was "Natural," as he was connected to the force and energy of Nature, really becoming that force itself, surrendering to it, flowing with it like the water within the banks of a river.....*

.....I closed my eyes and imagined rocking on the swing, higher and higher. As I reached the highest point, the swing slowed and paused for a moment. My heart seemed to follow the flow of the movement and stopped beating, in anticipation of great adventure. One moment, and with power and speed, I was plummeting down and rising back up. Hair dispersed by the wind, heart exulting in joy and excitement. A feeling of freedom and an unbelievable happiness seized me. "I am flying!" I opened my eyes. Sarah was patiently standing in front of me, waiting to receive the instructions.

"Close your eyes" I commanded her. "Imagine yourself on the swing, going higher and higher...." As I was guiding her through the imagery, I watched her body language and face closely.

"That's it! Yes! How did it make you feel?"

"I felt happy," she replied shyly.

"Why? What made you feel happy?" I asked.

"I felt free, flying."

"That's right! It was never about the swing, or even swinging. It was always about the experience of joy, freedom, and flying. In the same way <u>it is never about a double Salchow, or a double loop, or anything else you are working on. It is always about YOU and YOUR experience.</u> You may be confused by my words, yet please take a moment, turn around, and show me, where is this double Salchow you just did? Can you take it home with you? Show it to your friends? Wear it? Drive it? Eat it? Play with it? NO. Why? IT DOESN'T EXIST!!!!! All this time you were fighting for something that does not exist! Sorry, but it's true. So, what is this double Salchow then? It is an EXPERIENCE, it is an AWARENESS of your body, it is the strength of your spirit, it is a courage, it is a pure joy, it is an agonizing pain, it is a victory, it is a defeat. It is a journey to learn who you are. Finally, it is a game that we have invented through which we learn all the things I mentioned above. The techniques that you learned to execute this jump are only important as a map, a guide on how to get to your destination. You must realize that the point on the map that says "Los Angeles" has very little to do with "Los Angeles" itself. If you value the techniques (map) more than your own experience, you will probably not become the SKATING. You will be a skater, of course, as you already are! That is what we call a person who learns how to skate and practices the sport of skating for many hours a day. But, how do you cross that boundary between being a SKATER and becoming the SKATING? That happens when you learn to shut down your mind, your environment, your coaches, parents, other skaters, peers, fans, judges, ene-mies, and friends, when you completely surrender to the dance between your body and the movement, when you know that all that really matters is that EXPERIENCE..... Now, I want to see you "swinging on the really high swing". Ready? Go!"

She took off, picked up some speed, and prepared to jump another Salchow. I listened to my heart. Here came the familiar sensation of the suspended heartbeat. I held my breath, and in one instant, I felt something releasing within my-self, and then happiness, joy, and freedom. That's it! She did it! She smiled back at me, as we both knew that this time she did something meaningful, and I knew that I had not only found the key I was looking for, but also the door it opened.

"Sarah, I want you to anchor this learning and remember what happened today during the lesson. Please, make sure you write about it in your weekly report." She nodded her head, and skated off.

I have so many of these reports collected from my stu-dents over the years. Recently, while eyeballing through some of them, the following phrase drew my attention: "Like sugar in a cup of coffee". The phrase, seemingly meaningless, flooded me with memories of another special lesson.

It was during the freezing morning session at one of the ice rinks I worked at for a time. I was standing by the boards shifting from one foot to the other trying to keep warm and teaching a student how to tune in to her body. She listened to me intently, wanting very much to please me and do exactly what I said. Yet this desire to please resulted in her putting forth more effort than needed and causing her body become stiff and uncoordinated. I asked:

"Listen to your body. *How does it* want you to move?" She was looking at me, and I could see how hard she was trying to figure out, *how did I* want her to move? This misunderstanding between us forced me to search for more creative solutions in the attempt to reach the common ground. I was getting cold and frustrated when her mother brought me a cup of Starbucks. As I picked up the cup, a vision formed in my mind's eye.

I saw myself sitting behind a long table along with 10 other people. I was facing a tall glass cylinder positioned in front of me. A paper spiral was hanging on the thin red silk thread inside of it. The spiral, adorned by the colorful design of my own making, hung still, protected from the outside forces by the glass. No talking, breathing, even moving, was going to disturb its peace. Yet, it was the task I had at hand—make the spiral spin without any physical connection.

I was attending a telekinesis seminar, and each of the seminar participants was curious as to whether or not the phenomena of moving objects by the power of one's thoughts was real or not. Each of us was sitting in front of the glass cylinder, each observing the spiral of his own making. I was looking at my spiral, silently sending it my loving thoughts and asking it to show me its tail. After a few moments, I found myself slipping into a strange awareness of becoming the paper spiral myself, hanging on the thread and spinning around. It appeared as if the separation of space between me and the spiral ceased to exist, and *we became one. At the same time my spiral started spinning. I couldn't believe my eyes! I turned right and left to see how my peers were doing, and I found that only one other person was as successful as I was at spinning his spiral at that moment. While I got distracted, my object stopped spinning. I tried to "spin" it again but without any success this time. I tried harder to concentrate, to no avail! It just wouldn't work. <u>I realized that trying harder and being competitive with others did nothing to move the spiral!</u> It was very frustrating, and frustration didn't improve my ability to connect with my object. I knew that there was something very different in the way I felt when I was able to move the spiral as compared to the time when I couldn't. And right then, it became very clear to me that we are not our bodies, that being an athlete and pushing yourself to do unimaginable tricks, it is, in part, telekinesis. When we dissolve and become the very thing we do, connected with the energy flow within us and around us, without being distracted by who is watching us, who is doing better or worse than us, or wanting to be better than anyone else, when we are pure and completely absorbed by the experience of doing, unaware of any possibility of a failure, it comes out perfectly, seemingly without any effort, naturally.*

"Think about a sugar you put into a cup of coffee. What happens to it?" I asked my student.

"It melts."

"Yes, and when it does, it becomes part of the coffee. They become inseparable, don't they? While the sugar is still in the cup, it ceases to exist on its own. It loses its own identity. We stop calling it "sugar," and we simply call it "coffee". That should become your goal: to dissolve, to surrender, to trust, to cease existing, to disappear, to become one with the movement. Let the movement and your body become your guide. Listen to it. Hear it. Follow it. Become it! Dissolve in what you are doing. Flow with it. The ancient wisdom of times is being stored within our bodies. Mmmmm. It is now so delicious! The combination of sugar and coffee, or ....mind and body."

She listened to me, intrigued and mesmerized, as I continued:

"Now, it is one thing to be 'in the mind', to understand the idea cognitively. As a coach I teach you ideas, but as a skater, you must "translate" the idea into the "experience". What exactly does that mean? As a coach I can find millions of ways to describe "sugar" to you, yet there is only one way to "know" sugar. It is to taste it, to experience it. While experiencing it, you must release all of my explanations of the sugar and realize what this sugar is like to you. *What does it taste like? How does it make you feel? What does it do to your body? How does it get absorbed?* You must take your time to learn "sugar". In the process of learning "sugar", you'll notice that you also learn about your body and your emotions. You learn about YOU! You learn about the relationship you have with Yourself! You become AWARE!!! You become AWARENESS!"

Awareness is like a flashlight in the complete darkness. You can't see a thing; you wander around, stumble and trip upon things in the darkness. It's scary not being able to see. Suddenly, you get a flashlight. While you still cannot see everything around you, you become capable to at least see what's in front of you, you become empowered to make choices. You can clearly see the roadblocks now, and you can effectively deal with them. Without awareness, you would continue struggling with unseen obstacles and falling into the dark holes.

"The best athletes have superior awareness, balance, and coordination," I heard Kerry Leitch, World and Olympic coach, saying at a seminar 20 years ago. His words etched in my mind, like a universal truth, and I made sure to remember what he said. Kerry was an excellent coach, and he taught excellent concepts. But it took me 18 years of coaching figure skating, researching, and extensive practice of yoga, tai chi, and meditations to *"experience"* what he was talking about myself and to be able to teach these ideas to my students effectively. The theory of "experience" and "awareness" is maybe one of the most important parts of this book. Why? Because everything else in our life is an illusion, and the only REAL thing is our EXPERIENCE.

Sure, it was very exciting to see the paper spiral spin, but it was the experience of oneness with it, the experience of losing the sense of separation, time, and space that made it so wondrous. It was in this experience of losing the sense of self, I became aware that everything already is; all the knowledge, all the stories, all of the past, and all of the future. Everything is already present, but it is hidden from us until we learn the component of awareness. It is in moments like this we become aware of our true essence, our power, our beingness, the

Presence of something greater than we are, the inspiration, and the muse. The paper spiral, or the double Salchow are only the metaphors that represent our relationship with the outside world. We fight for our independence, our specialness, our separateness, and control, creating misunderstanding and conflicts around us. If only we could realize that by releasing the attachment to our small self, relinquishing control over others and realizing the oneness with those around us, we could be on our way of getting the exact thing we want with ease and grace. We will achieve then a state of being nothing and owning everything in the process. We will experience ourselves as Divine Beings and will attain peace and joy in our lives.

> *"Live to learn to love.*
> *Learn to love to live.*
> *Love to live to learn..."*
> *~Rico Dasheem*

DOUBLE AXEL+DOUBLE TOE+DOUBLE LOOP PRACTICE

Once again I invite you to find a comfortable place to sit where you won't be disturbed. Sit with your spine erect and focus on your breathing. Notice how the breath enters your body through your nostrils. Feel the air touching the inner lining of your nostrils as you breathe in. Just really allow yourself to experience breathing like never before. Once you do, slowly get up and walk around the room, paying attention to all the senses engaged in a simple act of walking. Who is the person seeing through your eyes, hearing through your ears, coming into contact with the floor through the soles of your feet, feeling the skin of your body touching the clothing...

10

Combination Spin

It's in the attitude

"The longer I live, the more I realize the impact of attitude on life. Attitude, to me, is more important than facts. It is more important than the past, the education, the money, than circumstances, than failure, than successes, than what other people think or say or do. It is more important than appearance, giftedness, or skill. It will make or break a company... a church... a home. The remarkable thing is, we have a choice every day regarding the attitude we will embrace for that day. We cannot change our past... we cannot change the fact that people will act in a certain way. We cannot change the inevitable. The only thing we can do is play on the one string we have, and that is our attitude. I am convinced that life is 10% what happens to me and 90% of how I react to it. And so it is with you... we are in charge of our Attitudes."

~ Charles R. Swindoll

10

Combination Spin

It's in the attitude

"How is your book going?" my friend asked me. I haven't seen her in a very long time, a few months at least. She was in hiding. I knew that she didn't want to be seen after going through difficult financial and family relations problems, and I didn't try to get her out of her hiding place.

Some people hide, afraid to be judged or criticized. Some hide because they don't like to be questioned and patronized. Some feel a deep sense of failure. Some just want refuge, to crawl into a cave like an animal and heal their wounds in solitude. I looked into her eyes and received a beautiful, loving gaze back. I was so happy to see her again and to give her a hug.

I could sense that she was still dealing with her ordeal, yet she didn't feel like revealing her pain to me as she asked me casually about my book.

"Pretty good, I think. As a matter of fact, I am on my way to the writing workshop right now. There I will get feedback on just how 'good' I am actually doing with my writing," I replied cheerfully, pretending as if I hadn't noticed anything.

"Do they read your work there?"

"No, I read it myself in front of the class, and then everyone is critiquing it."

"What will you be reading about?" she inquired. Suddenly, I sensed a possibility, and opening: to infuse her with an inspiring, empowering energy without the need to touch her sore wounds.

"The story I will read today is about the power of imagination. It is a story about the remodeling of my house, about having a vision of a Zen-styled sanctuary amidst the run-down, old-fashioned space..."

I had just finished writing this chapter several days before, and I was still under the spell of realizing how the ability to see beyond the problems, ability to see the potential hidden below the surface, helped me and others to overcome obstacles and reach success. If I could invoke the very same ability in my friend, what implications it could have on her future. I had to tell her the story!

"Would you like me to read it to you?" I asked.

"Yes! I'd love to hear it!"

I reached into my bag, pulled out several neatly printed pages with my story, and invited my friend to sit down on the bench. I sat next to her and started reading, carefully pronouncing the words and watching her expression. She leaned forward and listened attentively.

"The moment we crossed the crooked, shabby front door of the house, I saw it! It was my Little Spiritual Retreat. I sat down on the floor and closed my eyes...."

I read. My friend was listening intently, nodding her head in agreement. Encouraged, I continued to read my story until I came to the following paragraph:

"It was a long and somewhat painful process with many obstacles and hurdles to overcome. Yet at last, when we walked into our house for the move-in inspection, we were astonished by the beauty of the final product!"...

All of a sudden, my speech slowed down and my mind tranced out into another vision. In one moment I saw a movie of all the obstacles and hurdles that took place in the span of the six-month-long remodeling project. A **powerful insight** emerged from the depth of my subconscious, where it was hidden in the process of a transformation of the dream into reality.

"Is everything okay?" She noticed the change in my facial expression as I zoned out into my new vision.

"Yes, yes. I am fine."

"But?....."

"I just realized that this story holds another important message that I wasn't aware of earlier...."

"*The house was bought. As new owners we'd received the keys and the rights over our property. It was now time to decide what to do next: move in and put "makeup" on the wrinkled face of our "new" 42-year-old home, or postpone our move-in date and go for a major "face-lift" operation. Just like wrinkles on the aging face don't cause health problems to their owner, the old-fashioned construction and style of our house didn't mean that it was in unlivable condition. All the appliances and plumbing were in working order; the roof was weather-proof, and we could move in and live there just as all the previous owners had. But we didn't. We chose to go for a major reconstruction surgery, requiring knocking down the walls, rebuilding bathrooms, putting stuff in, and taking stuff out.*

We hired construction workers. With confidence, skill, and poise, they used their hammers, working in rhythm to contemporary R&B. By the end of the first week, only exterior walls remained intact, and our house, as we knew it, ceased to exist. It became completely unlivable with torn-down walls, ripped-out toilet, and all sorts of wires hanging from the ceilings and the walls. Almost every day I drove by to check on the progress of construction, looking forward to 'seeing' the improvements. Weeks went by, and there was no visible progress. Some days the workers were busy with other projects and didn't show up at all. Other times they worked on the inner structure of the house: electrical, plumbing, etc. It seemed to me that nothing was moving, and each day passed by, and our move-in day moved further away. The house was broken; nothing worked; no progress was made towards completion of construction, and workers were asking for more and more money to continue work. It was a test of patience, belief, and the ability to stay centered, calm, and present."

It made me think of all the skaters who came to work with me, having tried different techniques and methods. They were already accomplished and well-versed in skating dynamics, but for some reason could not achieve the results desired. I could 'see', what needed to be done, to break through 'the wall', the plateau, to go to the next level. However, it required a complete transformation, the result of which was temporary 'loss' of ability to execute conquered-already elements. Many of these skaters and their parents were discouraged by the slow process and a lack of vision. While focusing on the negatives in front of them, they couldn't handle the 'demolition and laying the infrastructure' phase of the process and moved on, searching for a quicker and easier approach with a different coach, one that didn't require "knocking down a few walls." They would put a 'makeup' on, 'gloss over' the problem areas and do okay for a while, but never be able to reach the potential that was in store for them, the potential that would bring lasting change and real results. No caterpillar became a butterfly, without going through the process of forgetting itself, forgetting how to undulate, and eat leaves, forgetting the life and the essence of a caterpillar...

Caterpillar....

"Hmm, how strange!" I thought, and moved about my chair, while rereading the words I wrote. "It's strange... but....I am a caterpillar!" I exclaimed in astonishment. Lately, I've been losing patience with myself and my book.

"I am a caterpillar!" I realized that it was my metaphor. I saw myself wrapped in the beautiful cocoon of my house, hibernating in my book. I squirmed on my chair because I still remembered being a successful caterpillar. I rolled the trees and ate leaves, befriended other caterpillars like me. Although we were competing for the same food, I believed that I'd have enough to eat because I was one of the fastest. I thought that I would be a caterpillar forever and worked hard towards 'Best Caterpillar' award. But then, things changed, and my vision of myself, my purpose had changed also. For some reason, I thought there was more to me than being a caterpillar. Even being an extraordinary caterpillar was not good enough. I retired and broke all ties with the caterpillar world. I went into my cocoon to create something different, better, grander. I was comfortable and warm in my cocoon, and I felt, making progress towards that, that was my destiny. I didn't miss my caterpillar days. However, often I made no progress at all. I would lie down in my cocoon, warm, comfortable, and lazy. I began resenting myself for being so passive. I could feel that gradually, I started losing my wriggling skills and ambition. Fear and worry entered my heart. What if I forget, completely forget how to squirm? That was one skill that I was so good at. I never intended to sit in the cocoon forever. What if I forgot how to be a caterpillar when the time came to get out of the cocoon? What would I do then? How would I survive?

A doorbell rang. I opened it. There was Suzie, my friend. She extended her arm towards me with a gift bag. "Happy birthday," she said. "Thank you so much!" I took a bag. I put a smile on my face, but inside I felt broken and lost. What was I? I was no longer a caterpillar. I was this lazy thing that sits all day in the cocoon and does nothing of value. I judged myself. I couldn't even remember why I chose to go into the cocoon in the first place? What was I thinking? I reached inside the bag. There at the bottom, wrapped in the colorful tissues, lay something, something heavy and meaningful, I could tell.

"It's for your desk," said Suzie. I held the object in my hands, feeling its weight, pausing the unwrapping. In the spur of the moment, for no apparent reason, I remembered a story that happened to me some time ago.

My body was standing next to Donna's, demonstrating tai chi moves she didn't understand, and my mouth was blubbering the explanations. She looked confused. I felt irritated. She was looking for the teacher's clarifications, and I was looking for her to go away and leave the teacher with all his attention to me. No one asked for my help, and I felt stupid and angry for volunteering. Besides, I didn't want to help her at all, other than to help her out. Donna was new in this class and needed instructions, but I perceived her as a pest invading my space and stealing my teacher. She had done that before on many occasions. In other classes and events, I had the pleasure of enjoying them with her. And now she was here, doing what she always did, taking all the attention on herself!

The class was over, and I went home. The heavy feeling gripping my heart went home with me. I knew that even though the class was over, the lesson was not until I found the resolve to the real issue triggered by

Donna. I felt resistance. My mind wanted to say that there was nothing wrong with me. It wanted to point a finger at Donna and say, "It's all her. She is noisy." Yet my heart knew. If there is no issue, it can't be triggered. I sat down, grabbed my journal and a pen, and started scribbling as fast as I could. My teacher's voice echoed in my head, <u>"Every issue is an opportunity for healing. When you are 'upset because', look for projection."</u> I shook my head, got up, and headed towards the refrigerator. There I was going to find my comfort food. It would help me deal with my emotions, I hoped. I reached for the shelf where I'd hid some cheese. But my cheese was gone. Not a single crumb was left! My husband ate all of the cheese. How dare he eat it all! I had no choice but to return to my desk and dive into my issues. As the black ink appeared on white paper, organized by my thoughts into the words and sentences, the puzzle of my upset with Donna came to life. I wrote:

"I am the one who loves receiving my teacher's attention. If someone else is receiving it, I don't get enough.

I love cheese. If I don't eat it fast enough, someone else will, then I don't get enough."

*It went on and on, and I found **that most of the things that I was doing in my life were motivated by the fear of not having enough.** I worked so hard to try to prove to the world and myself that I was good enough. I was afraid, thinking, what if another coach was better than me. What would that mean? I am not good enough. What if someone gets some recognition? I would not get enough recognition, or not enough money, or not skinny enough, or not smart enough.... Whatever it was, it was not enough! I was determined that I have to do whatever it takes to make sure that I have more than enough of everything. And then I realized that the* *biggest one of all not-enoughs was my fear of not having enough LOVE, that I somehow believed that love was only available to the ones who were good enough, successful enough, smart enough, etc. And then, right then, I knew, that I AM ENOUGH! Regardless of the number of wins of my students at competitions, or how much money I was earning, or how much recognition I was receiving. None of those things were making me more or less. I AM perfect, exactly as I am! I AM ENOUGH!*

It was such an incredible revelation that I just wanted to sing, dance, and hug everybody! Most important, I wanted to hug Donna for showing up on my way, and teaching me this lesson. I felt so liberated because I knew now that of all the things I was doing out of fear of not being or having enough, I could now do for the pure pleasure of doing because I wanted to, because I love it, because it's FUN, and because I CAN! And I also learned that I can't fail! Right then, I remembered a quote by Robert Schuller

*"What would you do,
if you knew, you couldn't fail?"*

I smiled to myself.

"Open it!" Suzie's voice entered my consciousness. The unwrapped gift was still in my hands. Slowly, layer by layer, I started removing the colorful paper concealing the contents inside. There was a clear glass heart, with a convex top and flat bottom. A picture of a beautiful butterfly was drawn at the bottom of the heart! Of course! How timely! 'I am enough' no matter what, and it's okay to forget the caterpillar way of living. "Thank you, Suzie, for reminding me of the butterfly in <u>my</u>

<u>heart</u>!" A feeling of gratitude filled my being. I was no longer a caterpillar. I was not a butterfly either, not yet! But the magic of metamorphosis had begun, and in time, I would experience the joy of flying. I would learn to fly in time. That is the truth, and it's my choice to stay conscious, present, and grateful for the place I am in right now. There was a shift in my attitude, and immediately I felt not only empowered, but inspired....

The feeling was strange and exciting all at once. Nothing had changed in my life at that moment, yet everything changed. I reached out to the bookshelf and pulled out an old dictionary.

> *"Attitude-* \'a-tə-,tüd, -,tyüd
> — *n, the way a person views something or tends to behave towards it, often in an evaluative way."*

So simple and clear, our behavior will lean towards the direction of a chosen attitude. "The way a person views something," shows up in the way a person approaches life; it shows up in his words, thoughts, and behavior. Attitude determines the meaning we assign to things and events around us. Attitude is the invisible force directing one person to be grateful for the event and another person to be upset about it. Attitude can have an incredible effect on one's life. It is a life force that can make us or break us.

Once, in a Performance Mastery workshop I wrote six polar opposites to each other pairs of words on the wall:

Succeeding or Failing,

Laughing or Crying,

Winning or Losing,

Praising or Punishing,

Encouraging or Criticizing,

Appreciating or Taking it for granted,

I asked participating students to choose the part of the pair they liked. All of them chose the first part of each pair, of course. Then one girl raised her hand and threw out, "Sure! You need to talk to my mom about it, or my coach. They are never happy with what I do. They are constantly yelling and criticizing!" She appeared frustrated, almost angry. I looked at the other kids, and most of them were nodding their heads. I smiled empathetically.

"I know what you are talking about. I, too, had a 'skating mom' and a coach 'from hell'. However, today I'd like to talk about YOU. How do YOU treat yourself? Are you treating yourself any better than your coach or your mom, who seem to only see the mistakes you have made?

How do you treat yourself? When you fall on the attempted jump, what is your response?

How do you treat yourself? Do you give yourself a pat on the back and words of encouragement, such as, "I know you'll get it! I believe in you! You can do it! I've seen you overcome more challenging obstacles," or maybe something like this: "Good job! I am so proud of you for taking a risk and trying! I know you will soon land this jump with more precision, when focused on.....[correction]." Is this how you treat yourself? Or do you silently get up off your butt, swear through your teeth, and look around for the offender? How do you treat yourself?" I looked at the kids, and they sat silent, thinking.

How do you treat yourself when you land a jump? Do you acknowledge and praise yourself or take the effort for granted?" I heard a low whisper echoing my words: "Take the effort for granted." I nodded; over the years I've trained many athletes and observed their immensely critical, self-deprecating behavior repeatedly. I have also observed almost immediate results of their destructive thought patterns.

I closed my eyes and instantly pictured a former student, a talented girl who was expected to join the ranks of the most elite athletes in the world one day.

I could see her going for a challenging triple jump.

I could see her hesitant, doubtful, not believing in herself.

I could see her poorly timed jump attempt resulting in a meaningless pop.

I could see that she didn't commit herself to the execution of the element.

She didn't commit herself to the discovery of her true potential, or the possibility of a failure.

She didn't commit herself to the possibility of greatness.

She loved winning, but hated losing more

Popping a jump for her was neither a defeat, nor a waste of time.

Popping a jump for her was neither a lost opportunity, nor a disgrace.

Popping a jump for her was an unconscious habit, although a conscious choice.

Popping a jump for her was not an inadequacy; it was a coping skill to deal with fear.

She was not afraid to fall; she was afraid to fail.

She was afraid to learn that she wasn't good enough.

She was afraid to face her unworthiness.

She was terrified of rejection. By choosing to pop, she was in control of the outcome.

She shook her head, as if she is displeased with the resulting pop.

She shook her head. However, I knew that consciously or unconsciously, she put on a skillful act of 'looking' upset.

She shook her head.... Why? Because she believed that everyone was expecting her to behave that way, or else she might be yelled at and punished. She believed that everyone would think that there was a valid fault with the technique, or the ice, possibly another skater getting on the way, distracting from the completion of the jump. She believed that if she convinced everyone in her act, she would convince herself that somehow she was better, worthier, as a result.

She skated over to me and we talked about her attitude, beliefs, and the importance of commitment.

She appeared to be listening, taking the information in.

She appeared like she would attempt the next element. There was still insecurity lurking through her eyes, and I sensed unnecessary tension in her body, but she went for the jump and launched herself into the air. Three revolutions later, without any attempt for a successful landing, she crashed onto the ice. The look on her face spoke volumes. Yet I clapped for her. I saw the approaching victory nearing, step by step. I had a vision.

How many want to fail? No one. How many want to succeed? All. What is blocking her way to success?

It was imperative that she knew what she wanted.

It was imperative that she believed in herself.

It was imperative to develop inner awareness and confidence.

It was required of her to praise and acknowledge herself for courage, acknowledge herself for taking the next step towards discovery of her potential.

It was required of her to take responsibility for herself and for her attitude.

It was required of her to get clear, focused, present, and calm.

I communicated this to her, but in her anger, she couldn't hear me. Her inner voice was louder than mine.

She was angry.

She was angry with herself.

She was angry with me,

Angry with her mom,

Angry with the world.

She thought that by blaming herself, she was acting responsibly.

She discovered that by blaming herself, she avoided being blamed by others.

She didn't understand that by blaming herself, her mind went into the search mode for finding everything that was wrong with her.

She didn't understand that by blaming herself, she gave her mind permission to find an appropriate punishment. She will find what she is looking for! We always do! She misunderstands the meaning of the word "responsibility": ability to respond.

There will be a few more pops coming her way and a few more falls. Her anger will rise higher, and her falls will pain her body more, providing the punishment she believes she deserves. In fact, she is always in pain, always injured. Eventually a moment will come when her inner voice will yell, "Enough! Just do it!" and in one instant, a decision and a commitment to act will form. "Enough! Just do it!" She will land the jump. "Enough! Just do it!" But she doesn't realize how, what happened, where did the command come from? She mistakenly believes that a successful jump rises from the anger that consumes her. Her angry ego changes its tune and turns into relief: "Okay, I am not a complete failure."

Unfortunately, she didn't learn the lesson. Unfortunately, she will avoid attempting this element again. Unfortunately, she knows too well that she will have to go through the same roller coaster ride all over again:

Pop, fall, pain of self-punishment.

Pop, fall, pain of self-punishment.

Pop, fall, pain of self-punishment.

Day after day, week after week, year after year.

No one seems to see the pattern.

Wheels are spinning.

Merry-go-round.

Dreams are being dreamt.

No one wants to wake up.

We keep repeating the same mistakes.

The story plays in my mind, yet it is an absolutely true story. This skater is not alone in her war with herself. Every competitive training center, rink, golf course, court, concert hall, school, business, corporation has a number of these competitors. Many of them are sitting on the sidelines, waiting for the healing of their repetitive injuries, perhaps looking for a new partner after another breakup, or a new job after a layoff.

Tons of people have learned to accept injuries as part of the sport; they are not.

Tons of people have learned to accept accidents as part of life; they are not.

Tons of people have learned to accept disease as something inevitable and expected; it is not.

Plenty of "competitive" skaters and parents mistakenly assume that they are competing (or really being in a war) with other competitors. That is not the case. It really becomes the war with yourself, and if it is a war, then there must be a winner and a loser, a hero and a victim.

But if this war is with yourself, can you really win it?

If this war is with yourself, what is the benefit of winning?

If this war is with yourself, what are you risking to lose? Is it worth it?

My role model, idol, Indian leader, and mystic, Mahatma Gandhi, was quoted as saying:

> *"The law an eye for an eye*
> *makes the whole world blind."*

If this war with ourselves leaves us "blind" or injured, what did we really accomplish? There has to be another way. A way where an ice rink becomes an arena of learning, joy, and self-discovery. It doesn't mean that we will have to be happy all the time. That is not realistic.

But it is completely realistic to look at ourselves and our mistakes with appreciation and understanding.

It is completely realistic to be grateful for all the mistakes and obstacles along our way for teaching us awareness, responsibility, perseverance, and commitment.

It is completely realistic to be grateful for the assistance of these obstacles in moving us forward, if we allow ourselves to see it that way.

It is completely realistic to see there is really no war. It is just an illusion, and as such, it contains no losers. Everyone wins the prize of their respective learning.

...I am lying down on the huge, soft sheepskin rug in the middle of my living room. Gazing out at the full moon and stars, shining through the skylight, warmed by the soft light of the flickering candles, I am breathing deeply in tune with the sound of falling water into the koi pond. I look around me, pleased by ambient feel of my gorgeous house. I feel happy that we chose to break it down and reconstruct, that I held to my vision, that my patience paid off, and my doubts cleared. It seems unequivocal to me that in order to move forward to the next level in life, or any area of life, it is necessary to **break through the place of comfort and certainty, then discomfort and uncertainty.** Only the ones who can endure both cycles with patience, grace, presence, vision, and purpose, and do it many times over, have a chance to attain mastery, wisdom, get wings, learn to fly, become a champion. While we think that we want comfort and peace in our lives, have no problems, we soon discover such a life to be boring and to resemble a 'dead zone,' a zone in between of not-too-happy and not-too-unhappy. Suddenly our peace is disturbed by some drama. Challenges pop out on our way, prompting us to dig deeper, to create solutions, to solve problems. Humans were designed in the likeness of their Creator. The gift of creativity is given to us for use. Once we fall asleep into a dream of comfort, we lose our drive and ability to create. We lose our purpose. It appears, though, that we have a choice to wake up on our own and break through the comfort zone (such as choosing to rebuild) or be propelled into the sea of the uncomfortable unknown by the events in our lives over which we have no control, where everything seems to be breaking down. We can also choose the attitude with which we'll live through these cycles.

No caterpillar became a butterfly without going through the process of forgetting itself, forgetting how to roll and eat leaves, forgetting the life and essence of a caterpillar...

In gratitude, embrace and surrender....

COMBINATION SPIN PRACTICE

In your next practice session I'd like you to examine your attitude and see if you can turn it around. Allow yourself to remember a recent event where you were upset about someone or something, a person or an event. Write down all the reasons why you are absolutely right about being upset about this. Once your list of 'becauses' is exhausted, ask yourself, how did this event serve me? What was good about it? What could I possibly learn from it? How can I benefit from this situation? Be honest. Once you've finished, read both of the lists. Which one will actually help you to move forward? You are now empowered to choose. Acknowledge yourself for the work. Offer a gratitude prayer for the lesson.

11

Triple Salchow

Resist not fear!

Imagine yourself standing by a beautiful, crystal-clear, calm lake, shimmering in the middle of the night. You look into the dark water and see a shiny, bright white full moon. Beholding it, you imagine knowing this moon. Do you really? Is there a moon in the lake? Or does it just APPEAR to be the moon? The real moon has a completely different structure, size, composition, texture, quality. How often do we mistake our fears and perceptions for reality, and then go after the "moon in the water" rather than the real moon?

11

Triple Salchow

Resist not fear!

"I heard you have fire-walked, is that true?" someone asks me. I smile and nod my head in response.

"Wow! Did it hurt? Did you burn your feet?" This question always follows, and when I reply that it didn't hurt at all, I receive looks of disbelief and an exclamation, "I could never do that!" While I enjoy the status of a 'super hero' very much, I want to negate, "Really?! How do you know that? What else have you chosen not to try only because you 'knew' ahead of time 'how badly it <u>would</u> hurt and that you could <u>never</u> do that?'" Of course, I usually keep quiet, and just smile in return. Yet, I thought, what an important subject for exploration!

"Sam, I see you are struggling with a triple loop. Why aren't you landing any?" I finally ask a skater. I'd observed for a while. He was repeatedly throwing himself into a jump without any attempt of landing, crashing mercilessly on the ice.

"I haven't really been working on them," he replied.

"Am I understanding you correctly, that to land your triples, you must work on them for a certain amount of time?" I am puzzled, but his head makes a slight downward movement in acknowledgment.

"May I ask you, what is the <u>right</u> amount of time, before you are <u>allowed</u> to land it? And who is going to 'allow' you?"

What stands in one's way and dictates in a clear voice, "You can't do that?" Why do we choose to listen and obey this voice without ever questioning its validity and or the validity of its command? Who or what is standing behind this authoritative voice? Why are we allowing it to run our lives? Make our decisions? Choose our actions? Create our destinies? Why do we identify with this voice?

The answer to my questions arrived as if in a dream. Faint as an echo, I heard, "I was afraid, afraid, afraid." It reminded me of the lesson I once had with my sweet nine-year- old beginning student - Diandra, learning to execute single jumps.

Diandra was standing before me with tears swelling up in her huge blue eyes as she confessed, "I was afraid." Only moments earlier I asked her to pick up the speed, embody the feeling of ownership, and demonstrate a toe loop. She skated out with excitement, joy, and a burning desire to do exactly as she was told. I was observing the beauty of an innocent determination, power, grace, and love emanating from her, as she was speeding up, cutting through the ice, and clearing corners. She was so exquisite in her commitment to do exactly what she was told to do. But as she turned into the preparation for a launch, all of a sudden her tiny body shrank, shoulders went up, and in one instant the jump was lost. She approached me with lowered head, and eyes full of bewilderment. "I didn't own it," she said disappointedly. I shook my head: "No, you didn't, but that wasn't the real error, Diandra, it was a RESULT of an important mistake. Think, what was the TRUE mistake?" I invited her to go deeper within herself, to understand. That's when tears started swelling in her eyes. Constrained, she looked down, and confessed:

"I was afraid."

"Yes, that's true," I nodded, "and I want to acknowledge you for the courage to own your truth. I also want to acknowledge you for a beautiful and powerful preparation going into this toe loop. Now, you have two choices here: A) let your fear own you, or B) own your fear. Which one would you like to choose?" She looked up at me, and smiled:

"I choose (B), to OWN my fear!" she said with conviction. I looked into her eyes, but she was lost in the fantasy world, imagining what it would feel like "owning her fear." Once she was ready, I encouraged her to go and repeat the jump. This time she looked super determined! I could sense her fear, but she went right through it, and nailed a gorgeous toe loop. Her face reflected a wide array of emotions she was experiencing. Her eyes were glowing with pure joy, and her smile was huge! She understood that the jump itself was not important, it was the break through the fear that had all the meaning! I thought of an inscription printed on the tag of the yogi tea bag I had that morning:

"Happiness comes when you overcome
the most impossible challenge."

It resonated so much with me at the moment! This was the kind of challenge the tea bag was talking about. I clapped and gave Diandra high fives.

"You had such a valuable lesson here! I can't even tell you how proud I am of you! Use what you've learned and do a loop jump now." Almost hopping, Diandra took off to prepare for the next jump (a newer and more difficult element for her), registering a now familiar look of determination on her face. A few moments later, she emerged with an excellent, powerful loop jump. My heart exploded in gratitude.

"Now, Diandra, were you afraid of doing the loop?" She nodded her head quietly.

"That's right. Only this time you owned your fear and went right through it! Awesome job!" I beamed. "Tell me, are fears of the toe loop and the loop the same or different?"

"Different" she responded without hesitation.

"Did these fears FEEL different?" I probed again. She thought for a moment.

"No, they felt the same," she replied, smiling at her realization.

"You are right. It doesn't matter what jump you do, the fear always feels the same. I must admit, that is very good news for you because, you are learning the STRATEGY on how to own your fear. You can practice this strategy again and again, until you OWN it completely. Soon, people will notice you and say, "This skater is FEARLESS." Only that won't be entirely true. Fearless people don't exist, to my knowledge. Everybody has fears,

although not everyone has a strategy on how to work with them. But you will."
She smiled ear to ear, and I felt fulfilled; the lesson was taught well.....

As I jotted down the story of Diandra's lesson, I thought about it again. Did I tell her the truth? Is it the truth that people without fears don't exist? What if some people didn't believe that fears are real? What if they believed that fears were just an illusion? Would they still have an experience of 'fear'?

Yes, I told her the truth the way I understand it in this time and space that we call 'now.' Fear is not a thing. It is a feeling that arises from seemingly nowhere unexpectedly and swipes the unsuspecting traveler's mind. The untrained mind falls for it and stumbles on the way, losing focus, direction, orientation, strength, and balance. Fear shows up in the form of a thought or vision, calling for an immediate physiological response that creates contraction, and tension, heaviness and discomfort. One cannot see it with the body's eyes, as it is part of an 'invisible world,' a world largely unacknowledged by people. They are too busy devoting their time and energy towards achievements in the 'world of form.' Many, perhaps, are just terrified to enter their Inner Space, filled with thoughts, feelings and emotions, and they would rather busy themselves with movements, TV, or mindless conversations, anything to silence the voice. Yet, there are others, who are like brave warriors, pick up a map of the unfamiliar Inner Landscape, where fear comfortably cohabits, study its territory, learn all of its residents, and with courage dive in into the darkest unknown.

They train their minds, and learn how to win over the master controller and saboteur of their lives - fear. And so they learn not only how to immediately regain control and use the energy of fear to their advantage, but transform it into love...

"Yin and Yang, White and Black,
Feminine-Masculine, Front and Back,
Fire and Water, Heaven and Earth,
Real and Magical, Death and Birth
Hot and Cold, Love and Fears
Take one out, and all disappears."

I once had a dream, a nightmare of sorts. In this dream I lived with my family on the 10th floor of a high-rise condo apartment.

It was evening, and my daughter and I were savoring our dinner, sitting in the dining room. A soft breeze was blowing into the apartment through the open door leading to the balcony. All of a sudden, I felt something seriously off. The hair stood up on my arms. I looked up, and above me, a white glass Japanese-styled pendant lamp started spinning wildly around the dining table. I grabbed my daughter's arm and pulled her towards me as we ran together to the kitchen. At the same time, the lamp got torn off the ceiling and flew diagonally across the dining room in the direction of the balcony, through the doorway, hitting the railing with such force that the railing bent on the impact. The lamp fell off the balcony and went down. I was terrified and speechless. I felt that the 'lamp' was after me somehow. Yet, I was also curious and wanted to see what was left of it. We slowly started moving back in the direction of the family room, where the balcony was. I peeked into the room, and there to my bewilderment, I saw all the wires from all the electronics dancing and twisting like snakes, trying to disconnect from the walls. It was like a scene from Poltergeist. I gave a cry, and called out to my then husband, "Dima, the house is possessed. It wants to kill us!" My daughter ran to him, but he calmly stood at his spot and told me to quiet down and that he couldn't see anything unusual. I realized that I was the only one seeing anything, maybe because the 'house spirits' wanted to kill me alone. It was my battle. I wanted nothing more than to keep my family safe, and so I decided to run to the balcony by myself, where the mysterious, aggressive spirits would hopefully follow me and leave everyone else alone. The wires freed themselves from the wall and rushed after me to the balcony. I looked directly at them and yelled, "Fine, go ahead and kill me if you want! I surrender!" For some reason I didn't believe, that it was going to go so far as to kill me, but I was wrong. In the next moment, I found myself being forcefully thrown over the railing. I was free falling off the 10th story! My heart jumped to my throat, and suspended its beat. In that instant a thought flashed through my mind that this is it. I am going to die. In the next moment my teacher's voice entered my consciousness: "There is nothing bad, only good. Show love no matter what you see or what happens to you." I yelled out into the air as I was falling, "I don't care. I love you anyway!" At the same instant a young boy of 17 to 19 appeared flying next to me, catching me in his arms, and saying, "Thank you. All I wanted was for someone to notice and accept me." Free fall stopped, and I found myself flying in the Spirit's arms. I smiled to his confession, and he asked, "Would you like to see the world where I live?" "I would love that!" The next phase seemed like a scene from the Disney's Aladdin movie; the flight on the magic carpet. We were in another world, a world so beautiful and enigmatic that I had tears in my eyes. I have never seen anything more admirable. He showed me his school, *gardens, home, parents, and teachers. I then somehow found myself awake and back in my own house, in my bedroom. I felt energized and refreshed, happy and fulfilled! I had a certain sense of faith, unshakable belief that I know now how to transform a fear. It is not through fight, not through ignoring, not running away, but through becoming fully aware of it, accepting, and loving.*

"Tell me a story of a girl who skates, Sarah." I was teaching another lesson, "Tell me what she feels and experiences as she picks up her speed getting ready to jump. Let everyone, who is watching you live through this girl's experiences, your experiences! Don't go for the familiar outcome. Don't go for what you already know." I taught Sarah and thought of Charles Lutwidge Dodgson at the same time.

Dodgson is better known as Lewis Carroll, author of a famous novel, *Alice's Adventures in Wonderland*. Thinking of him makes me wonder how did he arrive at the idea of a story about a girl who fell through the Rabbit's Hole? What is the Rabbit's Hole, and who are all the characters living there? I imagined Dodgson (Carroll) sitting at his desk, staring at a blank page for hours, but nothing would enter his mind. Feeling frustrated and lost, he decided to go for a walk in the park to escape the terror and agony of writer's block. It was a beautiful, sunny, warm, early fall afternoon, and Carroll was walking upon a green lawn covered by rustling yellow and red maple leaves. Suddenly, he stumbled upon the hole in the ground. His startled mind takes a flight of imagination and begins its famous descent into this dark, deep hole, when quite unexpectedly, it was interrupted by his friend's daughter Alice Liddell. Maybe he asked Alice, "Who do you think this hole belongs to?" "Maybe it's the rabbit's hole?" the girl said. "AHA!!! Hmmm...."

What happens next? He made Alice fall into the hole, into the dark, scary hole. At first, he had no idea what happened in the darkest holes of the invisible unknowns. How does she feel? What will she do? Who will she meet? We began to follow Alice, a girl, on the journey into the Dark Hole that actually turned out to be a colorful kaleidoscope of ever-changing adventures. He gave it a name, Wonderland. We experienced her discoveries, learnings, fears, victories, and defeats. We met her friends and foes, her opponents and supporters. We were captivated by the story, but more so by Alice and her unusual experiences. As Lewis Carroll unfolded the story, he really had no idea where it would land itself. He was just as captivated and intrigued as we were, the readers. The story is not about how clever Carroll put his words together. Who cares about that? What we are really interested in is how his character overcomes her obstacles, how she develops... How we develop through this character...

"Sarah, like Lewis Carroll, find out what happens to your character when she goes all out into the unfamiliar territory. Let her fall into the dark Rabbit's Hole of her feelings and thoughts. Allow her to discover the Wonderland, learn the map of it, become familiar with it. Master it! Rule it! Sarah, become an author of your story! Create magic! Become a book itself!"

As I watched her transform, I realize why we are so drawn to watch Nationals, Worlds, Olympics. It is not the perfection that captivates us the most, but the struggle of overcoming, break through the difficulties and fears. It is the "Hero's Journey," so beautifully described by Joseph Campbell, we secretly desire to repeat. But we allow the fear to rise above us and dictate, "I could never do that," without questioning if we are so afraid of it posing a real threat to us.

> "Through the firewalk I learned
> the trick our mind plays
> in unity with fear; it magnifies
> the illusion of pain tenfold.
> It plays the mental movies of the burning flesh, awakening the terror of the enormous pain.
> Yet, there was no pain, and human flesh
> was not at all at risk.
> The only burning that there was:
> attendants' hearts on fire,
> consumed by the desire
> of breaking through..."

Yes, the statement I am making here is: the fear of the event we are afraid of, is highly exaggerated by our mind. The actual experience, once accepted, is very mild. Yet, there are some rules, I recommend to apply. These rules worked for firewalking, but seemed universal enough to be applied in any area of life.

1. Don't stop to think; you will burn your feet. Timing is everything. (I am sure, many can relate to this one: problem of over-thinking!)

2. Don't run; take one step at a time! Rush, and you might find yourself tripping. Falling on your face into the fire-heated coals, will hardly improve your appearance.

3. There is no turning back. (Well, you could go back, of course, but the hot coals are now in front and behind you. In other words, no matter which way you go, there is a level of pain. But, I am afraid, the pain of going back way exceeds any imaginable pain that may/or may not lie ahead.)

4. Don't look down. If you do, the image of glowing red hot coals, will undoubtabedly reactivate 'fear,' making it difficult to follow rule (2). Looking ahead and slightly up, while repeating and imagining the words: 'cool moss,' 'cool moss,' 'cool moss' will help you to stay calm, and not feel any pain. Imagination is a powerful tool, useful in any high-pressure situations.

Now, you may want to ask: "What purpose do our fears serve? Is there a purpose?"

I don't know, but it seems that only fear can present us with the experience of courage, heighten the pleasure of breakthroughs and accomplishments. It is the most powerful emotion that can bestow upon us the opportunity to deeply experience self-love and self-compassion, and the knowing of the limitlessness of our being.

TRIPLE SALCHOW PRACTICE

Every time we are aiming at stepping out of our comfort zone, we experience emotions we call fear. Sometimes its grip causes us to freeze, procrastinate, blame, get angry, or simply give up the journey. Whatever coping mechanism we use, we tend to avoid facing our fears. In this exercise, I'd like to invite you to look at the recent situation where fear was a factor in making a decision. Let yourself feel it once again. Allow yourself to be uncomfortable in this emotion. Now, just sit with it. Notice where in your body fear resides. Imagine that this fear is a little child, scared, crouching in the corner. Come and sit with this child. Put your arms around her. Comfort her. Allow her to feel your love. Notice how the little one begins to relax. Mentally tell her that she is not alone, and you will always be with her, protecting her. Keep your promise. How do you feel now? Would you make the same decision or a different one?

12

<u>Double Axel</u>

Enter the Zone

"I didn't pay attention to times or distance,
instead focusing on how it felt
just to be in motion,
knowing it wasn't about the finish line,
but how I got there that mattered."

~Sarah Dessen

12

Double Axel

Enter the Zone

I was sitting on the four-way stop intersection, waiting for my turn to pass through. The time was moving slowly, giving me more space to think about my book. I just finished a previous chapter that I felt was a great success, but now was consumed by writer's block, unable to decide what I needed to write about next.

"There are signs everywhere to help you find your way," all of a sudden I remembered the quote from the movie *Fools Rush In*. "Thank you for reminding me," I said out loud to my wise subconscious. "You know that wherever I go, I always look for signs that can impact my writing and living."

"Outer experience is a reflection of your inner reality," my subconscious mind throws in a quote by my professor, Ron Hulnick. Another car passes the intersection, and I can now clearly see the red octagonal warning with a short, severe word: STOP. I put two quotes together and a clear picture formed in my mind. My inner reality was such that I was sitting still at the 'STOP' sign with writer's block, just as I was sitting at the 'STOP' sign in my car! As my mind focused on the red, octagonal symbol, I thought about the meaning and the purpose of this important traffic signal. It was not designed to stop us, it was designed to keep us safe, alert, and make us aware of any possible endangering situations coming from the blind sides of an intersection. It brings a driver's attention into focus, perhaps refocus. It is not a time to turn off an engine or check emails and texts on the smart phone. It is time to re-center and get ready to continue the journey, leaving the past in the past, and concentrate on the now. We all go through the stop sign intersections. However, not all of them bear the red octagonal symbol to remind us where we are and what to do with it. They are the "checkpoints" in our lives. They come in different shapes, colors, and events. Yet, recognizing and having a strategy on dealing with them could greatly improve the success rate on every level of our being. It is here, where the most important competitions of our lives are either won or lost.

January 26, 2012, San Jose. U.S. Figure Skating Championship, or "Nationals" for short. It is the premier event in the country, where crowned medalists receive a sought-after opportunity to represent the U.S. at Worlds and Olympics, along with the coveted title and status of a National Champion. I was watching Senior Ladies' Short Program, the first segment of a highly competitive event, which would conclude with a challenging Long Program a couple of days later. A newbie, Agnes Zawadzki, rose to the top. She gave a performance of her life, all she had. The excitement took over as she realized the possibility of seizing the moment, the moment within her grasp. She was not yet a crowned champion, but she arrived in the first position to the 'STOP sign': a one-day break before the next segment of the competition. In front of her lay a golden opportunity, a test for true mastery. I wondered if she could remain focused, unattached to the results, or would she stumble, unable to bear the weight of expectations...

> *"When an archer is shooting for nothing*
> *He has all his skill.*
> *If he shoots for a brass buckle*
> *He is already nervous.*
> *If he shoots for a prize of gold*
> *He goes blind*
> *Or sees two targets–*
> *He is out of his mind!*
> *His skill has not changed. But the prize*
> *Divides him. He cares.*
> *He thinks more of winning*
> *Than of shooting–*

And the need to win
Drains him of power.
~The Way of Chuang Tzu

Unattached to the results, one can experience greatness.
Like deja vu, I remembered helping Sasha Cohen prepare for the Nationals in 2006. Was it in St. Louis? It slipped out of my memory. That was not important. She won the Short; it was awesome! It was her chance to finally get the crown she had worked for, for six long years. Each year so close to victory, and yet so distant. Each year the win was within her grasp. She could almost feel its touch, then an inevitable strike of the mistake would leave her off the highest position on the podium.

My heart was not beating as I was watching the longest program ever. I was watching from the stands, sitting in the middle section, in the center, some 30 rows away from the ice, close, but not close enough. My attention focused on the JumboTron. The giant screen TV towering above the arena, detecting the slightest movement of an athlete. She skated to the center ice, hands on her hips, shrugged her shoulders to let go of the extra tension, and took her starting position. The whole huge sports arena, filled almost to capacity with appreciating fans, fell silent, expectant, as if everyone was holding their breath. The glove I held in my hand slipped to the floor and was patiently waiting to be picked up at the right time, but not now. The camera moved for a close-up of Sasha's face. I searched her face for an answer. "How is she feeling? Can she do it?" She was fighting a horrible flu. I felt guilty as it was my flu that she caught, but I already recovered, and she was still struggling with hers. She was so petite, so fragile-looking in her beautiful gold-toned dress. Where was she finding all her strength? Her makeup was perfect, her lips slightly parted, eyes looking far and nowhere all at once. She moved into her zone, the slight state of trance. She came here to win, and she was readying herself to go through each move methodically. I could feel her breathing, her vulnerability, her fear, and her prayer. Yet, there was also an unbelievable strength within her, shining through her eyes and palpable in the preparation pose. Her energy was gathering in the center of her core, ready to fight. It must have been a moment, but it seemed as an eternity. At last the music started playing. Sasha moved her hands up and took a powerful first push into the opening three turn. "Romeo and Juliet" was playing in the background, but I didn't hear it. I was so intent on watching every little detail of that program that I knew so well. I felt as if she was moving through it in slow motion. Was it really that slow? I couldn't tell. Was the Triple Flip two-footed? It went in such a blur that for a moment I thought I dreamed it. No, they played it in a slow motion, and it was fine. She did, however, step out of a Triple Toe/Triple Salchow sequence. She didn't fall, but I died a thousand deaths in that moment.

There was a huge attachment to the result. It was not an ordinary Nationals. It was a qualifier to the Olympics, and the stakes were high. The stress surrounding the preparation was enormous! No wonder we both got the flu. Our immune systems refused to defend us against the flu attack, being under so much stress. In the end Sasha won the title. She sat at the kiss-and-cry with her long-time coach John Nicks and smiled to the cameras. Her smile was weary. It was a hard-won victory. When the scores were announced, it was clear that she was a winner, with a huge score, her personal best. Yet, the look on her face was not the one of happiness of achieving a long-fought-for goal, a dream come true. It was a smile of relief, of letting go of the pressure. Her victory was sweet, yet, bitter-sweet. It wasn't perfect. She allowed her thoughts to run away, even if only for a brief moment....

Tomorrow, there would be no room for mistakes, and young, talented 17-year-old Agnes, new princess-wanna-be, knew it. There was a lineup of hungry competitors breathing down her neck, ready to take over at the slightest mishap. Was she ready? Could she keep her mind steady and emotions cool? Could she stay unattached? Tomorrow would tell.

I looked out into my meditation garden. Powerful Santa Ana winds wildly swung my beautiful Goddess tree and bamboos. Everything seemed to be in crazy motion; swinging, swaying, twisting, threatening with destruction. The whole world seemed to be completely off-balance. Yet, something was drawing my attention, fascinating me as it had never before. Under the Goddess tree sat the majestic statue of gray stone Buddha, completely oblivious to the turmoil around him. The statue was put there to remind us of peace and tranquility, of the clear mind, and the wisdom of ages. As I continued looking at it, I noticed how it was at odds with the uproar around it. The inner peace was always present within no matter what was happening outside. The pandemonium in the meditation garden reminded me of the world we humans deal with on the daily basis. It made me think again of Nationals or Worlds, an important competition, where there is so much involved and things change on a moment-to-moment basis. It seemed so natural to us to swing right and left with the gusts of life, but was it the way to win or achieve mastery in the Worlds?

> *"The Master sees things as they are,*
> *without trying to control them.*
> *She lets them go their own way,*
> *and resides at the center of the circle."*
> *~ Lao Tsu*

I remember Brian Joubert skating his Long Program at the Worlds Championship in 2009 in Los Angeles.

I was watching live in the Staples Center. Brian, like Agnes, was first after the Short Program and hungry to win the title of a World Champion. The energy in the arena was in its apex. It was wildly vibrating, swinging up and down, right and left, producing whooshing sounds. Evan Lysacek, the American skater and local, just skated his personal best, flawless interpretation of Bizet's Carmen. *His performance brought the fans to their feet in the wild excitement and appreciation of the human spirit and athleticism. Hungry fans were ready to jump on their feet again, caught in the wave of the energy of excitement. Brian Joubert was next to skate. Pale, coming onto the ice, terrified of making a mistake, fully aware of the standing ovation for a rival, and the consequences of an unfortunate mistake. The fans were holding their breath, knowing that Joubert was a challenging competitor of their favorite, Evan. Joubert was prepared to fight with the quadruple / triple combination, a weapon that Lysacek didn't have. Step by step Joubert did it. The warmed-up crowd went more and more wild with each executed trick. The end of the program neared, and with it, Brian's difficulty of the elements took an easier turn. The last jumping pass of the program was an easy double Axel. Brian was pretty much done by now, flawless, strong performance. The win was almost guaranteed. He skated briskly past the Citizen Watch advertisement posted on the white of the arena's boards. He prepared to jump: back outside edge, swung his arms, stepped forward, and launched up into the air. The un-thinkable happened right then when suddenly he opened up and fell flat on his stomach. Brian was completely disoriented, tried to get up in a hurry, slipped, and fell again. With his fall his hope for a high position on the podium was slipping as well. Someone took a picture of his fall. The close-up showed the unfortunate Brian lying on his stomach in front of half of the Citizen watch advertisement. Only the last three letters remained in the background: ZEN, and Brian in front of it....*

What is the difference between a champion and the second best? It's the ability to be still in the mayhem of the meditation garden, when everything wildly swings and only a calm, centered Buddha sits peacefully in its center, in the ZEN.

January 28. The day when the winner of Senior Ladies event will be announced. It was Saturday, and I was spending the evening with my family: dinner out, then musical theater. Eliza Doolittle, a Cockney flower girl, was demonstrating her talents onstage, dancing and singing the famous "Wouldn't It Be

Loverly", while dreaming of a better life. I distractedly followed the plot of the play, more interested in checking the results of the parallel battle going on at the same time in San Jose's HP Pavilion.

As soon as the intermission lights went on, I reached for my iPhone:

Safari

Icenetwork.com

Events and Results

scroll down

2012 Prudential U.S. Figure Skating Championships

Click

View Results

Click

Events: Championship Ladies

Status: Final

click, click, click.

I knew this procedure very well. I had performed it many times in that day alone.

Nineteen ladies were scheduled to compete in the order of lowest-scored skaters after the Short Program performing first, highest-scored last. Angela Wang's name showed up at the top of the list. She was currently in first place with a high combined score of 158.66. Not bad at all. I was impressed. Her Short Program effort didn't produce a desirable outcome for her, and she was only 16th coming into the final part of the competition, more than 17 points behind the winner. She had to skate very well that night to redeem herself, but there were still eight more skaters to go, Agnes among them. I sighed. It would be another hour before the event's end and I'd find out Agnes's fate. To earn the crown of the National Champion, she'd have to kick off the 'Champion's shoes,' she'd been 'walking' in since Thursday. Would she be able to do that?

The curtain went up, and the second act of "My Fair Lady" begun. Higgins and Colonel Pickering at the center stage celebrated Eliza's triumph at the ball. "You Did It" they sang in exultation, believing whole-heartedly in Higgins' success, both completely oblivious of Eliza's presence in the room and of her feelings of being used, abandoned, and ignored. Only when Eliza flung Higgins' slippers at him in anger and disappointment was Higgins confused, realizing that something was off. As the second act was unfolding, I'd noticed the hidden message in the musical beautifully correlating with the unfolding drama on a different stage several hundred miles away. Here, Higgins won the Short Program segment of his 'competition': Eliza's stellar performance at the Royal Ball. 'Sitting' at the 'STOP sign' after the ball, he didn't leave the past in the past. He continued to dwell on his success, missing focus and perspective of what was really important. The result of his carelessness was the possibility of failing the Long Program': losing the love of his life.

An hour flew by, and the show ended. Actors stepped onto the stage for the final bows, receiving a thunderous standing ovation, then disappeared backstage. The lights went on, and I was able to check my iPhone once again.

Safari

Icenetwork.com

Events and Results

scroll down

2012 Prudential U.S. Figure Skating Championships

Click

View Results

Click

Events: Championship Ladies

Status: Final

click, click, click.

The competition was now over, and Ashley Wagner, a seasoned competitor, claimed the 'Shoes' and the 'Crown' of the National Champion for the first time in her life. Since I didn't see the event, I could only guess what happened there by reading the competitors' scores. I scrolled down the list to find Agnes' name. Her placement revealed a huge presence of anxiety, fear, doubts, and expectations. I am sure the commentators said that Agnes lacked experience or something to that effect. She fell twice and stumbled on several jumps. Costly mistakes put her in seventh place in the free skate, one below Angela Wang. Yet, Agnes still managed to take home the bronze by carrying enough points over from her perfect Short. Not bad, but I am sure she felt disappointed, if not with her placement, with the poor performance. Only one day did she get to 'wear' the 'shoes of the National Champion,' while dreaming of the crown...

I reached into my purse and pulled out an old, worn-out copy of Tao te Ching, my never-failing guide and inspiration. Eighty-one short, poetic verses summarize the timeless wisdom, speaking to the heart of the willing reader. I opened it at random, and the following verse confirmed my thoughts:

> *"Success is as dangerous as failure.*
> *Hope is as hollow as fear."*
> *~Lao Tzu*

Hmmm, success, failure, hope, and fear are no ordinary words. Like demons, they are hiding in the dark corners of our inner selves, ready to come out in time and tempt us off the path. They are the ghosts of past and future, and there is only one remedy that can save us from another painful lesson: Stay in the present, here and now.

"Imagine yourself in a beautiful soap bubble. It's clear and flexible, shimmering with iridescent swirls. Nothing can enter this bubble without your permission. Don't make eye contact with anything! Even the walls have eyes, and can pull your attention from being focused on your center-self and your task," I instruct my students. "Once in the soap bubble, its light and airy essence will carry you, in its own unique current, and you will almost float above the ice effortlessly, as if weightless."

The mysterious flow channels my words as I am teaching, filling me with unique feeling of love and joy. I need not to think where they come from, just trust....

My iPhone made a dingy noise, alerting me to the in-coming text message. Automatically I glanced at it to check the 'intruder's' identity, and in a wink of an eye I lose my focus, the here-now, and my flow.....

I lose....

"I lose an umbrella.

I am seven. It's my mom's favorite umbrella,

new, automatic, with the button on the handle.

It came from a faraway country,

cost a 'fortune'.

She told me...

It was raining. My mother took me to the circus.

I love the circus! I was completely occupied by the performance.

The clowns were the best! I remember their act...

Maybe I can be a clown when I grow up, and make people laugh.

I put the umbrella on the seat right next to me.

It was getting late, and I was tired.

The dimly lit circus, the burgundy-velvet upholstered seats and walls, the smell of the elephant's manure, long day of skating before that...

All these were lulling me to sleep.

We left the circus, and the umbrella.

We walked outside onto the dark Odessa street, smelled fresh and clean after a summer thunderstorm.

My mother yanked my hand, prompting me to run quickly to catch the bus to the hotel where we were staying.

The bus was crowded with the circus spectators.

"Where is the umbrella?" my mother asked.

My whole being filled with terror. The righteous anger of my mom will strike like a powerful tropical storm. I will be black and blue for my absent-mindedness.

I shrank. I wish I was a turtle, hiding in the safety of my shield.

She called me names, I cried. Does she really love an umbrella more than she loves me? I wondered.

I wish I didn't leave it in the circus.

I wish we didn't go to circus.

I wish I didn't make my mother angry,

I wish she stopped humiliating me in public,

I wish......she hugged me, and told me: "I love you."

I wish.....

What more could I wish for?

I feel sorry for myself.

She hates me, I bring her pain.

Only bad girls bring pain to their mothers, and lose things......

Lose focus......"

"It's too hard." My six-year-old student Layla brought me back into the present. "It's too hard to be focused all the time."

"It is, Layla. That's why we need to practice. But I don't want you to use the word 'hard.' Let's change it for 'challenging,' and see what's going to happen." I suggested an alternative: "It's challenging to be focused all the time."

"What's the difference? 'Hard' or 'challenging,' it's hard either way!" She dismissed the suggestion impatiently.

"Yes, I agree with you, it does seem that way, but I still want you to use the word 'challenging.'"

The use of words is very important. Words affect our physiology, direct our focus. You say a certain word, and with it comes the meaning and the feeling. You are either energized or drained, empowered or deflated.

"Layla, let's do an experiment," I proposed. "Close your eyes and repeat the words "it's hard" a few times. Stir in a little bit of an attitude into the mixture, and notice how it makes you feel inside your body. Notice the weight on your shoulders, as if someone put a bag full of big gray rocks on your back and asked you to carry it with no destination in sight. It's soo hard, and heavy!!!! Notice how overwhelmed and tired you are. That is all you can think of now. Each big gray rock is a problem. Problems are so hard, and there are so many of them. There is no time to fix them, and they pile up one on top of another, more and more. Very soon, your back starts aching, and you just want to put this bag down, and walk away from it." She shifted from one foot to the next, adjusting her position. "'Challenging,' on the other hand, brings with it a mixture of something exciting and empowering, something to overcome, something that will prove your ability and strength. Visualize these two words: 'Hard' as a rock, a boulder. It is big, gray, and immovable. There is no way to get it out of the way; it will always be there. 'Challenging' is like a big chunk of ice, although it's dense like a rock, It can melt when you warm it, when you hold it in your hands, when you sit on it, when you keep it close to your heart." A huge smile appeared on her face. "I get it!" she exclaimed. "When I work on something 'challenging' and love it, the 'challenge' begins to melt away like the ice. It becomes smaller and smaller, until it disappears!" "Exactly! And you can actually watch it disappear!" Layla never stopped surprising me with her precocious wisdom. "Remember I told you the quote: *"Energy flows where attention goes?"*" She nodded. "So, what are you going to focus on now?"

She took a deep breath in, centered herself, taking great care to see that every part of her body was in exact alignment, stepped into the "iridescent soap bubble", and skated off to pursue a long-sought-after dream of one day wearing a crown of a National Champion. What was her destiny, I wondered? Would she be able to experience what she was dreaming of? Would she survive the many storms, obstacles, and setbacks waiting ahead of her? Would she survive the many successes? Would she learn to appreciate the beauty, meaning, and the purpose of the STOP signs on her way? Would she develop the ability to sit centered and peaceful in the mayhem of the meditation garden, called life, like a majestic Buddha in the ZEN?

DOUBLE AXEL PRACTICE

Many people today are either living in their past stories or worrying about the future. As a result of this unconscious practice, they miss the opportunity available in the present moment. Yogies are known to say that body follows the mind and mind follows the breath. Today's practice will be about conscious breathing in order to help you with bringing your focus into the NOW. I suggest you do the following practice for five minutes three times per day. Sit yourself in a comfortable position with your back straight. Close your eyes. Take a slow, deep breath into the belly, allowing your belly and your rib cage to expand. If possible, take this breath in five counts. Notice how it entered your body. Now hold your breath for 20 counts, paying attention to the sensations in your body. Slowly release the breath through your nose, counting to 10 as you are exhaling. The air will first come out of your lungs, then, with the assistance of your diaphragm, push the rest of the air out of your belly. Throughout the process keep your focus on your breath. If you lose your focus, no worries. Just return to your breath as soon as you caught yourself.

13

Combination Change
Foot Spin

Transformation Happens

"Just because I liked something at one point in
time doesn't mean I'll always like it, or that I
have to go on liking it at all points in time as an
unthinking act of loyalty to who I am as a person,
based solely on who I was as a person. To be loyal
to myself is to allow myself to grow and change,
and challenge who I am and what I think. The only
thing I am for sure is unsure, and this means I'm
growing, and not stagnant or shrinking."

~Jarod Kintz

13

Combination Change
Foot Spin

Transformation Happens

Wednesday morning. I was facilitating our usual session with my client. She was sitting on the sofa cross-legged, looking out the window. Her eyes were cheerless, but her face perfectly composed. Her carefully slicked-back hair was pulled into a neat bun. She was dressed casually in white nylon jogging pants, white t-shirt, and a baby-pink sleeveless pullover, and I was intrigued by this deliberate attempt to control, and a hint of carelessness. What would our session be about today?

I closed my eyes and saw an image of her in a monastery, dressed in all black overalls. I looked more closely:

"Did you ever want to be a nun?" I asked out of the blue. She looked at me in disbelief.

"How did you know?"

What could I say? I didn't know. It was just an image that flew uninvited into my awareness. Where did it come from? Should I always say what I saw?

The conversation had now taken on a different form. Something clicked inside her that brought memories. Her eyes filled up with tears.

"I don't understand what is happening to me. I am so weak and lost. I don't know what to do. The worst part is that I don't really know what I want anymore. I used to be so strong. Everyone came to me for advice. But now......" Her arms moved, as if they wanted me to see this despicable mass sitting on the couch. Tears were flowing down her cheeks.

I heard her pain and despair. So many people fall into this trap, the race for the results, achievements, things, stuff..... then void. That question rises up from the depth of a soul: What for? Why? Things start falling apart, stuff becomes unimportant, and then comes the moment, when the hour of glory became history. Only glimpses of it still remind us of that time gone by.

The mind is an odd mechanism. Engaged in the race for achievement, it is focused on the future. It lures us into a sweet dream of promising dazzling results. It forces us to run faster and faster, threatening with the image of coming in too late and missing the opportunity because, there in the future, there isn't enough for everybody. So go, my friend! Hurry up! Happiness is only available on a first-come, first-served basis.

Wasn't that my race too? Next student, next competition, next program, Regionals, Sectionals, Nationals, Internationals. Like a bottomless pit it was sucking my life out of me. There was no stopping. One more push and the happiness will be right there, waiting for me behind that next turn.

> My daughter was born, and turned one,
> Then two, then three, then four....
> Her nanny was fantastic and proud.
> She told me: Your daughter's so cool!
> How fast she was learning things.
> I listened to her absentminded.
> No, I am not absentminded,
> My mind's time traveler,
> Designing the formula how
> To beat competition, to win competition,
> And make my competitors bow.
> As soon as I get there, I'll catch up with my daughter....
> My dog dies of cancer,
> My dad dies in a car accident,
> Race continues, nothing will stop me.
> I train Sasha Cohen,
> I train another national champion,
> I am training pairs at Europeans....

My event was over. I stopped, caught a breath, looked around.... There, I saw European and World champions, world-class elite competitors, creme de la creme of the sport, dancing like puppets on the strings to the fiddle of the head of their Skating Federation, together with athletes, their coaches dancing the same dance. The president, fat and flabby, red-nosed from the excessive alcohol consumption, hanging on his beautiful 18-year-old anorexic wife, sparkling in diamonds, dressed in a sable fur coat, holding the magic strings to the athletes and their coaches in one hand, and scissors in another. In one easy motion, he can cut the strings, and the all-powerful, accomplished super-star athlete will turn into the nothingness, they came from. I felt sick to my stomach. I realized that my race had no end. My life was being sucked out of me, and there was no reason. "Why? What is the purpose in this race?"

My daughter is nine....
Nanny is gone....
My husband threatens divorce.

I reached that place of a dark hole, where the mind cannot see the future any longer. The vision was obscure and dark. The mind kept trying to find a way. It clung to the idea of "keep going." Only it was fruitless, so it turned back and looked at the past. It regretted. Or.....

Thursday. Next client.

Same story:

"I feel the change coming into my life. I am scared, almost paralyzed with fear. I can't sleep at night! What happened to me? I used to be so strong and successful?" Her voice trembled. Her body, reclining on the sofa, was stiff from the tension, hand pressed tightly against the chest. The severe look of her eyes was locked on a point somewhere far away.

That morning I picked up a card from a deck of Tarot, and it was #13, a card of Transformation, or 'Change.' A woman was drawn on its face with a look of panic in her void eyes. *"A time of endings is close at hand..."* read the description of the card. The author of this deck found a kind way to soften the traditional name of the "Death" card with a more uplifting substitute, such as in 'Transformation.' However, regardless of how the card was called, it is a milestone we go through in life. Attached to our past, we're afraid to let go. Just thoughts of change make our stomachs twist and turn. "You have the strength, as Transformation Card asks you to have courage and to know that renewal follows every conclusion."

In my beautiful office, sitting on the black leather revolving chair, I was taking a dive into another black hole, getting my client out. I now knew the road. I knew where they were. I knew how they got there.

"I used to be so strong..."

I want to scream: "Can't you see? You are not 'used-to-anything.' You are still here, completely intact, perfect, as perfect as ever, strong!"

But instead, I nod and ask, "Do you mind if I share a story with you?"

She nodded, "Please do."

"One beautiful Sunday afternoon I took my daughter to Petco to pick out a colorful koi for our newly build pond. We were very excited! Once at the store, we quickly headed off to the aquarium section of it. There were over a dozen aquariums filled with all sorts of fish of different shapes and colors. As we marveled at the beautiful species of marine life, we got approached by a salesgirl ready to answer our questions.

"May I help you?" Her appearance in front of us was very welcome.

"Yes, please. We are looking to buy some fish for the fresh-water pond." My daughter broke into a smile. The salesgirl took us to the corner and pointed to the six aquariums filled with a school of baby koi and baby goldfish of various sizes. Even though the selection was not super exciting, we were still thrilled to pick out our lucky four pond inhabitants. We felt certain that our fishes were very 'lucky' to leave behind Petco's boring one-foot-deep, two-feet-long glass aquarium which they shared with 50 other orange companions. Our champions were relocating into the new, luxurious accommodations of the pond. We pointed out the chosen four to the salesgirl, armed with a small hand-held fish net. Artfully, she fished them out and placed them into a plastic bag filled with water. Our 'lucky koi' didn't seem to share our delight and certainty that being taken out of the aquarium was the best thing that could happen to them. They looked confused and scared and clung to each other for comfort. I could only imagine their terror at that moment. They had no way of knowing that they were on the way to new discoveries, growth, and

opportunities. I hurried home, looking forward to stopping the suffering of our new pets. As soon as we got there, we released them into a big, beautiful pond where they were expected to establish a happy habitat and grow from 2.5-inch-long fries into full-grown 24-inch koi. As they slipped into the water, we anxiously waited for them to swim around. But they didn't. They dropped to the bottom of the pond and hid under the rocks. It seemed that they stayed at one small spot of the pond for months, scared to move. I would often joke that my fishes thought that they were chickens. Yet, regardless, they grew a little bigger and stronger daily. Eventually, they became confident with their surroundings and finally accepted our pond as their home. Now they had a real opportunity to reach their full potential and become who they really were: a 24-inch-long beautiful koi. This could have never happened to them if they remained in a two-feet-long aquarium with 50 other fishes. Some of those fishes died, never reaching their full potential. They endured existence, never knowing what it means to thrive, grow, and swim around as they were destined to. However, to grow and mature, live fully, they would have to be exposed to being taken out of the comfort of the familiar and cozy little aquarium, and put in a scary, big place that seemed to have no edges or limits, in a place where they had to find out just how far they could really swim."

My client's face lit up with hope and understanding. I smiled. No wonder Japanese consider koi as a symbol of strength and resilience to overcome obstacles. There is even a legend about a koi transformed into a dragon...

"Imagine for a moment your friend or a child feeling weak and hopeless, feeling scared. What would you do? Would you offer them help? Would you know what advice to give them?"

"Yes, absolutely!"

"Now, I am that friend in trouble. What would you tell me? How would you lift me?"

As she started speaking, I could see the spark in her eyes, chin lifted, and shoulders pulled back. There was more energy and strength in her body and enthusiasm in her voice. I gently interrupted and pointed out to her that she was her own friend in need of advice, and there was no one better than she to offer it. She then smiled widely; the "victim" exited the stage, and "Hero" returned. This was a glorious moment. She realized that she was not defeated. In that moment she came to the understanding that the "hero" and the "victim", the weak and the strong, both lived within her. It was not a question of "What happened to me? I used to..." It was a question of, "How can I tap into the "Hero" self again?" It is an empowering state in which one feels like she can do anything and deal with any change life throws at her.

At this moment, I asked my client to get up and walk around the room, repeating short incantations, sinking them into the depth of her heart:

"I am strong", "I am empowered!" "I am resourceful". "I am strong", "I am empowered!" "I am resourceful". "I **am** strong", "I **am** empowered!" "I **am** resourceful". "I am **strong**", "I am **empowered!**" "I am **resourceful**". **"I am strong", "I am empowered!"** "I am **resourceful**"!!!!!!! As she chanted incantations, I felt confident that now she had a stronger foundation to carry herself through the new 'beginning' that was awaiting her.

COMBINATION CHANGE
FOOT SPIN PRACTICE

We get bored with monotonous activities over a period of time. Yet, change may be scary and uncomfortable. Often, it brings anxiety and worries, but change is inevitable. Nothing ever stays the same. To help you better navigate through the changing waters, I'd like to invite you to look at the situation from the point of view of your friend. What advice would you offer to a friend going through similar situation? What would change in your life if you, yourself, chose to follow this advice?

14

Flying Camel Spin

Stepping into the Vision

*"When I let go of who I am,
I become what I might be"*

~Lao Tzu

14

Flying Camel Spin

Stepping into the Vision

Okay, it's time to come out into the clear water and face my own fears and insecurities. Time to be honest with you, my reader. It only seems fair. As I was writing this book, sharing stories with you, we became so intimately connected. I took you on the journey through the desert in Arizona, firewalking with Tony Robbins, explored telekinesis with Natalya, brought you on the trip to Italy, introduced you to my family and my fish. You sat through the lessons with my students, learned the inner game of double Axels, and experienced the pains of growing up in the former Soviet Union. And all the while, as I am guiding you on your journey to find the meaning and purpose in your own life, find the way to awaken the great dragon of your potential, I, too, am searching for my own answers for my own truth. I began writing this book as a figure skating coach with the intention of inspiring my readers, to go further, to achieve their dreams, reach the potential lying within. But in the process of this work my own transformation happened. A transformation I resisted for several years.

Next sentence needs to come out,
But I resist its writing.
Maybe I'll do it tomorrow.
I pause; 'It will not run away.'
I know, not to rush,
Once it's out, I can't take it back and stay.
Is it a right decision?
Is it a right timing?
My koi fish are clear.
But I still have doubts and fear.

Yesterday, when I went to the rink to teach my students and choreograph the program, I was sure in my decision, but once I arrived and started the work, the clarity evaded me again. I enjoyed teaching my students so much! There is an unbelievable strength and beauty in them. Their complete trust and surrender to me is so precious and vulnerable! It takes supreme character and strength of heart to trust another being so unconditionally, and I accept my position of leadership they gave me with gratitude and humbleness. I love teaching. I see a great potential being awakened within my students, and I feel very responsible for their progress and their journey.

My late mother wanted me to become a figure skater, a champion. She loved figure skating all her life. The truth is, I didn't, not really. I never wanted to be a figure skater. The two things I wanted to become were a teacher and an actress. The two came together in the place where I love telling inspiring stories! I loved telling stories in such a way that my listeners would hold their breath and wait without a movement for the next word that would come out...

Here I am again, trying to squeeze the words out of my mouth... The words feel like they are soap bubbles, a foam, a thin soapy film that forms in my mouth and prevents the sound from coming out. This is ridiculous! I am not even talking, I am writing! Does it really matter? It doesn't. Writing or talking, this is my experience, and no one is going to tell me that I don't experience that! You know how they tell you what you feel or how you SHOULD feel? Bullshit! No one can tell you how YOU feel! You are the only one who knows that!

"Wow! You have a bad attitude, my friend!"

"Oh, yeah? So what?! Do I always have to have a good attitude? I never did sign that paper where I gave guarantees to be a saint forever. I am not a saint! I don't want to be one. I want the freedom of having a bad attitude and throw in a tantrum when I feel like it!"

"You know, yesterday I saw the news that police in Florida have arrested a six-year-old girl for throwing temper tantrums."

"So? I am not six, and my temper tantrum is on paper, in perfect silence! And besides, it's not a surprise that someone has realized that sometimes it's the grown-ups who need protection from the badly behaved children! Where was I? You have interrupted me! Oh yeah, - I sat down to tell the truth, to make an announcement, but instead, I am talking all this crap about the irrelevant stuff.... I finally get it! It is my body that holds me back and doesn't want me to write the words."

"Are you serious?! Why not?"

"Take a nap" it says as soon as I want to write my critical sentence. "You are tired and need to sleep."

"Sure, but you said the same thing yesterday, and the day before, and the day before that too!" I told my body back, "Right at the time when I managed the courage to make a decision to finally just accept it and write the truth, I listened to you and took those naps. Do you remember what happened next? Nothing!!!! I never came back to write it again! You are playing the same trick on me! Why should I listen to you this time? You just want to sabotage my decisions!"

"Okay, let's be serious. You have doubts. If you didn't have the doubts, you would just do it. You wouldn't linger around. You wouldn't listen to anyone. You would be clear and enthusiastic. I am assisting you with giving you more time to sort things out. You are about to "jump off the cliff". Don't you want to be absolutely sure that this IS the jump, and that THIS IS the time to do it? You always make your decisions so quickly. Your whole life is about to change. DRAMATICALLY! Take my advice. Take a 10-minute break and clarify your intention. See your vision again. Make sure it is clear. I am your body! Why would I want to support you in making a bad decision? I am on your side, okay? Go now. I'll wake you up in 10 minutes. I promise!"

"Fine, then! But I am telling you, this is the last time I am listening to you if you don't wake me up and if I don't write anything when I come back."

"Okay, okay. Go now."

Off I went. Ten minutes came and went, and here I am back at my writing. A thought crept in that I really do need to wait with writing my announcement. What the heck? In a few minutes I will have to move my butt off this chair, and get myself ready to go to the rink. This whole week seems like a kaleidoscope. Scenes change so rapidly that I don't have any time to adjust to them, to figure out who and what I am, what I am doing, what's the purpose? I feel like I am sitting on a chair and someone from behind is pushing it in the direction of their choice. My legs are too short and cannot reach the ground to have any control of the direction we are moving into, or at least use my legs as speed breakers. We are going faster and faster, and I feel as if I am just going to scream: "STOOOOP!" I don't like going so fast. I am losing a sense of my center....

Center. Peace. Focus.

Stay in the moment.

I am here and now.

Here and Now.

HERE and NOW....

"Who am I?"

"A writer."

"Really? When did I become one?"

"Now."

"Did anyone ask me if I wanted to be one?"

"Did they have to? You picked up a pen and started writing. If you are writing, you are a writer."

"Yes, but now I have to go to the rink and be a skating coach!"

"Yes. You are a skating coach."

"Didn't you just say that I am a writer?"

"Not when you coach skating."

"It's so confusing! Why do you confuse me so much?!"

"But it's quite simple. It is not who you are. You just wear your identities like a mask at a carnival."

"Like a mask at a carnival?" I echoed the words, instantly changing my attitude. A memory of a dark, old Peruvian shack came to my mind.

I saw myself sitting on the worn-out, thin mattress, thrown on the floor in the corner of a small, dark room filled with the smell of the burning grasses. Several people, mostly Peruvians, gathered there, each sitting on a similar mattress, expectantly looking at a medicine man standing in the center. He was dressed in traditional, colorful Peruvian attire and an old felt hat. Carlos was his name. He smoked a pipe and explained to us in broken English the healing ceremony we were about to take part in. I heard about ceremonies like this and was curious to experience it firsthand. Carlos was brewing some tea made of local plants and offered each of us a cup. I took a sip, and the substance turned out to be very bitter but smooth. I grimaced. Carlos looked at me and smiled. I looked around and noticed that everyone had finished their drinks already. "This is what I wanted to do. No one forced me to come here," I told myself. I then took a deep breath in and finished the drink. Carlos nodded his head in approval and suggested I lean back on the pillows and relax. I did. Suddenly, I felt light-headed and dizzy. It was a funny feeling I had never experienced before. I remembered Carlos telling me that this was the ancient Peruvian ceremony where one learns what he specifically needs to know about life. Silently I set an intention, asking that whatever I need to know would be revealed to me. I opened my eyes. The room was still only dimly lit, but somehow it looked different. No longer was it old and shabby. It appeared as if everything there was a stage set for a cartoon, and people who were sitting on the mattresses took the appearance of the clay marionettes with painted faces. "What is that supposed to mean? What kind of sense do I have to make out of this?" When in the morning we got back to our hotel, I was still puzzled by my experience. Later that afternoon we took a walk around the old part of historical Cusco. A store caught my attention. "Let's go in here." I pulled on my husband's arm. It looked like a Peruvian art shop. On the walls there was an array of painted clay masks. I sighed. Those were the painted faces I saw the night before at the healing ceremony.

The memory of this event had often visited me, always with the same question: "What do I need to know about this?

Why was this revealed to me?" And now my body tells me, *"You just wear your identities like a mask at a carnival."* "Is **It** talking about the same masks I saw in Peru a couple of years ago?" I wondered.

"You have hundreds of them, and you change them, like clothes." My body continued, "If the weather is cold, you'd be wearing a coat. If it was hot, and you are at the pool, you'd wear a bathing suit. Funny, but it never occurred to you to call yourself a 'bathing suit', just because you are wearing one."

I still have not written that sentence, THE sentence that has stacked in my throat for several days now. Yet, something significant got clarified during this time. My body was so right to make me wait and linger and not rash into the inevitable.

My critical sentence was about the announcement I was preparing to make that I am retiring from coaching competitive figure skating and committing full time to my life-coaching practice. This seems like a huge decision to make, and just like that cut the ties to my past, to the incredible amount of work that I have contributed in my career, all the successes and all the knowledge. But it's true, *changing careers is not about changing who I am, it is just a matter of changing a mask.* Then what's the big deal about it? Exactly! I had to understand this concept before I could commit my decision to paper. Perhaps that was a meaning of the lesson revealed to me in Peru. As the awareness of my realization settled in my body, I got flooded with love. I don't know, I can't even describe this experience properly, but I started feeling this love, not as an emotion, but as a vibration, a high vibration of loving energy, the energy of creativity, and the energy of joy. In that moment I realized the coveted prize of the "what do you want" question, and "what is my purpose?" and even "how can I contribute to the world?" had a simple answer. I want to be in that vibrational frequency all the time, and I want to share it with others. We enjoy doing what we are doing because it gives us that feeling. This energy empowers us, moves us, makes us feel happy, connected, loving, and light. It gives us the feeling that nothing is impossible. It puts us in the flow and keeps us in the moment. Once there, it makes us crave to be in this space again and again. And if it's lost, it makes us go on the search to look for it all over again. It is what makes us know what "I am alive!" means. *"Remember,"* I heard Carlos's voice say, *"here you will learn what you specifically need to know about your life."* And the understanding comes in that this vibration is who I am and who you are, and in the end, it doesn't really matter whether you are a skating coach, a writer, a life coach, or a bathing suit, there will be no fulfillment unless you find your way to connect with that deep source of love within you and share it with others.

I closed my eyes, and the vision of my future moved closer to me and became brighter. I was shocked, at how clear it was!

I am sitting at the table holding my favorite pen in my hand. I love my pens, always have, ever since I was a child! I am signing my first book, freshly printed, at the Professional Skaters Association's Conference. A long line of people is waiting to get my autograph, an inscription, and a word of encouragement and wisdom. I take a deep breath in and exhale. I am picking up the next book to write another autograph. My heart is skipping a bit. I am so proud of myself. I have finished this work of love, the work of inspiration. I've learned incredible truths and discovered some secrets. I am writing the next inscription, moving my pen lightly across the fresh, clean white page gently, letting the ink and my love get fully absorbed into this book. I really want to take this moment in, to experience it completely. I have earned it! Many years of intense work and learning and over two years of writing. This is my celebration! I set an intention to stay connected and grounded. In one hour I will leave this table, re-center myself, and be ready to present my subject of "Awakening the Sleeping Dragon" to the conference's audience.

I am ready for it! I can barely hold still! I am so excited now! The "rubber band in my throat" has snapped! I am ready to speak out, to share my truth! To energize and inspire! I have practiced my speech, but it doesn't matter now! It is written in my heart, and I will speak from it! There is so much energy! I feel as if I am an electrical generator. I could light the whole city of Las Vegas! That's the power of my dragon! My happy, joyful, filled-with-love dragon!

I am now ready to be called into the auditorium. I am being announced and called forward. I am walking lightly. I feel as if my body is weightless. I am enjoying the sensation. I am feeling so confident! My body is so healthy, radiant, beautiful, and light! My gorgeous clothes are fitting me perfectly! My energy is contagious! I am stepping up onto the platform and smiling. I have a voice! I am being heard! What an incredible feeling! I know what I want! I have it! I am living it! And it is perfect! I am looking down the aisle, searching for my family, and there they are, my soul-partner and my daughter smiling back at me with encouragement. I am feeling their strength *and support, their unconditional loving. I can never fail with them by my side! They are my blessing! We have the most amazing heart-centered relationship! I am so grateful they decided to travel with me for my first big event! A rash of excitement moves up my back.*

I am scanning my audience. I am seeing a young woman, practically a girl, sitting in the front row with her beautiful notebook and wide-open, expectant eyes. She is hungry for knowledge. She wants to be the best she can be. I am smiling to her. I am recognizing her as myself. How many seminars, workshops, conferences has it been? How many have I sat through and thought, "One day, I will be presenting as well. I, too, can do this." Maybe that should be my opening line after all....

FLYING CAMEL SPIN PRACTICE

As I finished writing the last chapter of my book, I realized that a new chapter of my life had begun. Perhaps, something new and exciting is opening up for you as well. I now want to invite you to grab your favorite pen and journal and write your own personal vision down. Create a situation you wish to experience a year from now and write it in the present continuous tense, as if it is happening right now and you are living it! Make it fun and believable. You are now living your DREAM! Let yourself grow wings and fly....

Some say that my teaching is nonsense.
Others call it lofty but impractical.
But to those who have looked inside themselves,
this nonsense makes perfect sense.
And to those who put it into practice,
this loftiness has roots that go deep."
~Lao Tzu

The Table of
Contents Decoded:

Translations of the Skating Language

THE MUSIC: *Choreography begins with the selection of music.*
As a choreographer, I usually pick the music that fits a skater's style, temperament, and ability level. The music has to be flowing, and has to have depth and dimension, slow and fast parts. To find the right piece that hasn't been overused by other skaters is a time-consuming process and involves many hours of listening to finally find that one piece that not only fits perfectly for the rules, but also inspires the skater. The music is a background and the mood for the program, like the soundtrack to the movie, like.... the bookcover to the book...

Opening Pose: *Every program begins with an opening pose.*

Not only the performance starts from the stationary position that a skater assumes before skating into her first move, but a choreography process itself begins from the same place. I usually place a skater in the middle of the ice, and as we play the music over and over again, the image of this opening pose, like a sculpture in the sculptor's mind, appears. We yet don't know how this program will unfold, and we are prepared for the unexpected.

The Theme: *Without a theme, there will be no tale...*

I love creating stories, especially drama. Each program has to tell something, carry a point, an emotion, and has to resonate with the skater. The process of creating the program cannot begin until this theme is discovered. Once the theme is in place, the moves come, and we are excited to see what will happen next.

Footwork, Steps and Transitions: There are well-distinguishable elements in a skater's program, such as jumps and spins, that are interlaced and connected with each other by various steps and transitions. That's where the story is actually told! While, the skater is not directly rewarded for each step, it is here that the most difficult part (mentally and artistically) is taking place. The skater must act, skate with the skill and precision, pick up the speed, and maintain a laser sharp focus, while performing difficult turns, dance steps, and maneuvers, keeping balance, and make it appear effortless.

Triple Lutz+Triple Loop: *A super difficult jump combination.*
The words Triple, Double, or Single preceding the name of the jump indicates the number of revolutions a skater must rotate in the air. Skaters perform individual jumps, or they group two or three jumps together. In this case it is called a combination jump. All of the jumps are landed backwards on the outside edge of the 4mm blade. It takes a great deal of athleticism, mastery of technical, physical, mental, and emotional realms, and thousands of hours of practice to be able to complete triple Lutz/triple loop combination. In today's figure skating only few women in the world are able to successfully land this combination in competition.

Triple Flip: *Another challenging jump.*
There are six different jumping elements in figure skating. They are awarded a number of points for their execution, depending on their difficulty. Triple flip is the second hardest jump in the ladies division. All of the jumps look exactly the same in the air and upon the landing, but differ in take-offs. While there are different ways of classifying the jumps, the easiest way to recognize them are by the two distinct subgroups: 'toe' jumps and 'edge' jumps. "Toe" jumps are distinctly launched into the air with the assistance of the "teeth" (toe picks) of the blade. Flip is one of these jumps.

Triple Flip+Triple Toe: *Second most difficult combination jumps.*
Not only this combination is very difficult, it gets physically and mentally harder to successfully execute the second combination jumps as the skater's strength and endurance exponentially diminishes as they go along. Not long ago only men were able to do triple/triple combinations, as they were considered athletically stronger. More women are now appearing on the world stage successfully completing this combination, although there are still only few.

Triple Lutz: *The last of the triple jumps.*
Most of the time jumps are being taught in the progression from first to sixth, from easiest to most difficult. Lutz is the last jump and considered most difficult. Like flip, it is a 'toe' jump, although it has a slightly different take-off. It receives the most points as a stand-alone triple jump. Some jumps in figure skating are named after the first skater in history executing it, and Lutz is named after Alois Lutz, an Austrian-born skater who performed it for the first time in 1913.

Double Axel+Double Toe+Double Loop: *Last combination jumps in the program.*
By the rules of modern competitive skating, skaters are permitted to do three jump combinations, one of which can have three jumps. Since the second and third jump in this combination are only two revolution jumps (doubles), it is not considered too difficult. However, when performed in the second half

of the program and the skater already completed six triples, this becomes a challenging athletic feat, and as such receives extra points.

Combination Spin: *Another intricate element.*
In Russian, spins are sometimes called pirouettes, taken from ballet, and are believed to be inspired by ballet in its basic form. Spins are beautiful elements of modern skating, where a skater must revolve centered on a single point on the ice in a specific position, usually on one foot. There are three distinct spin positions; upright, where a skater rotates in an upright position, sit, in a seated position with the free leg being held in front, to the side, or tucked behind, and a camel, where a body is stretched in an arabesque. Combination spin incorporates all/or some of the positions and their variations. Some variations require a great deal of flexibility. Skaters who can perform them are rewarded with the extra points for difficulty.

Triple Salchow: *Jump.*
Salchow was invented by the Swedish skater Ulrich Salchow in 1909. Today, it is one of the first triple jumps skaters learn to perform. Because of that, it becomes one of the most practiced jumps, one of the most consistent, and maybe a little bit neglected. Many skaters feel comfortable executing it in competitions. They often place it at the end of the program, relying on their ability to land it successfully, even when they are tired. It is an 'edge' jump, where the curvature of the circle

assists a skater with creating the rotational pull necessary to complete the required revolutions in the air. Salchow doesn't receive as many points for difficulty as Lutz, yet, it's nevertheless a difficult jump, especially when performed at the end of the program. Every jumping pass receives extra points for being in the second half the program. As a choreographer, I always strategized on the placement of the jumps, keeping in mind the current ability of the skater and her mental and physical preparedness. Knowing this information allowed me to 'budget' for the maximum point value.

Double Axel: *The King of all jumps!*
Like Salchow and Lutz, Axel is being named after its inventor, Norwegian-born Axel Paulsen, who performed this jump for the first time in 1882. It is also an edge jump and the only kind where the skater launches into the air facing forward. Because of that, it has an added half revolution to its rotation, and of course, added difficulty. In other words, double Axel is not a two-revolution, but a two-and-a-half-revolution jump. Many people consider the double Axel as the first triple jump, and they are right. The whole new level of difficulty begins with mastering it. It is not uncommon to take up to three years of daily practice to learn this jump, and several more years to become consistent with it. There are many skaters who gave up on the sport because they couldn't harness the complete rotation of this elusive element. On the cover of this book you can

see the illustration of the skater performing double Axel frame by frame. While all other jumps are optional in the program, double Axel is mandatory. It is not a coincidence why I chose double Axel for the chapter on focus, or being in the moment. It is a required element in any 'program' you do.

Combination Change Foot Spin: *Well, as you can tell now, this is a spin.*
The difference between combination spin and the combination change foot spin is in the changing of the foot. The skater first rotates on one foot, then switches feet in the middle of the spin, continuing on another foot. Just like in life, changes happen, but the spin must continue revolving, and preferrably the speed will not diminish but increase. The speed of the revolutions actually helps the skater to maintain balance and center. Once the speed slows down, the spin dies out.

Flying Camel Spin: *This program concludes with the spectacular spin!*
Spins 'fly' when the skater enters it with a jump. I envision my skater here 'flying' fearlessly into her spin with a spectacular Arabian, a jump that resembles handless cartwheel. She appears to be almost upside down in the air, but she lands effortlessly into a very stretched gorgeous arabesque, 'camel'. No, it doesn't look like a camel and has nothing to do with these noble animals, sorry. The name appeared around 1930s. Named after the Australian skater Campbell, her name got badly misspelled.

I love dramatic endings to the programs, mustering all the emotions, passions, love, energy into the final ending pose, all along knowing that the last chapter of this program is the beginning for the new one....

Suggested Reading

1. Adrienne, Carol. *The Purpose of Your Life.* New York: William Morrow and Company, Inc., 1998

2. Chandler, Steve. *Time Warrior: How to Defeat Procrastination, People-pleasing, Self-doubt, Over-commitment, Broken Promises, and Chaos.* Anna Maria, FL: Maurice Basset, 2011

3. Dweck, S. Carol. *Mindset: The New Psychology of Success.* New York: Balantine Books, 2006

4. Dyer, W. Wayne. *The Power of Intention: Learning to Co-Create Your World Your Way.* Carlsbad, CA: Hay House, Inc., 2004

5. Hicks, Esther and Jerry. *Ask and It Is Given: Learning to Manifest Your Desires.* Carlsbad, CA: Hay House, Inc., 2004

6. Hill, Napoleon. *Think and Grow Rich.* Los Angeles, CA: Highroads Media, Inc., 2004

7. Holden, Robert. *Authentic Success.* Carlsbad, CA: Hay House, Inc., 2005

8. Hulnick, Ron and Mary. *Loyalty to Your Soul: The Heart of Spiritual Psychology.* Carlsbad, CA: Hay House, Inc., 2010

9. Millman, Dan. *Way of the Peaceful Warrior.* Novato, CA: HJ Kramer, 2000

10. Mitchell, Stephen (Translation). *Tao Te Ching.* New York: HarperPerennial, 1988

11. Redfield, James. *The Celestine Prophecy.* New York: Warner Books, 1993

12. Waitzkin, Joshua. *The Art of Learning: An Inner Journey to Optimal Performance.* New York, NY: Free Press, 2007

13. Walsh, Neale Donald. *The Complete Conversations With God, an Uncommon Dialogue.* New York: Hampton Roads, 2005

Acknowledgements

With my deepest gratitude and pleasure I would like to acknowledge all the people, who directly or indirectly assisted me with writing of this book.

First in Spirit of Gratitude I must acknowledge one person, I always forget to say "thank you" to is **mySelf**, for determination and commitment, strength of heart, discipline, for dedication to learning, and desire to improve. For being kind to myself, and always encouraging and empowering.

Next, it is my late parents: **Gita and Valery Kovler**. Without you I wouldn't have been who I am today. In many ways, you have provided me with inspiration, and taught me invaluable life lessons, not only directly, but on many subtle levels. I am still learning from you. Thank you.

Abbie, you are my wise advisor, and patient listener! Thank you so much for your help and support! I am so lucky to have a daughter like you!

Marina Zusman, my second mother. I am so grateful for all your love and support! I truly feel like my mom is looking after me through you. I love you so much!

Lyova Munitz, my beloved late uncle. How can I ever forget your loving support, guidance and gentle encouragement? You are forever in my heart!

Dima, for being my pillar, for feedback, and shoulder in times of need, and of course for a beautiful illustration for this book! I am grateful for you being part of my life, and for all the lessons you've taught me and continue teaching me.

USM, Mary and Ron Hulnick, your guidance in my life is immeasurable. I am so grateful for your teachings of Spiritual Psychology, the principals and methods of which, I use in my daily life. Without it, this book, wouldn't have been written, and I wouldn't have stepped in into the light of knowing who I am.

Steve Chandler, my mentor, for teaching me to be a Time Warrior, Wealth Warrior, a Giver, and a Server.... Your lessons are forever in my heart. You truly walk the talk, and inspire me so much! I am in deep gratitude to Spirit for putting you on my path! Thank you so much for all you've done for me and the success of this book.

Christopher Connolly, my coach, for pushing, pulling, inspiring, and holding the Light for me in difficult times, for cheering and celebrating every win, for holding the vision, and for believing in me and this book when I was loosing faith.

Jack Grapes for challenging me to become a better writer, for not giving me a slack, or an excuse. You pushed my writing to a new level, I didn't even know was there. I loved your Method Writing workshops!

Shelly Greenhalgh-Davis, my super editor and supporter! I've enjoyed working on my book with you. I always had confidence that with you by my side my expression will find the best way to come through, even when I couldn't organize my words into flowing sentences. I feel so blessed to have find you! Thank you for all the hours, love, and encouraging feedback you gave me!

Mark "Dr. Dream" Peebler, for showing up at the right time, for love, for helping me create "my dream" at a higher level then I was willing to hold for myself. With your assistance I pushed myself for more! I will always think of our sessions when *Choreography of Awakening* hits a 'best-sellers' list ;)

Bonnie Jarvis and Kathleen Weidner, my Angels, who just stepped up to help me just because! You are some of my greatest teachers! It is through people like you, I know that there is something invisible behind each one of our backs, who is infinitely loving, caring, guiding and protecting. Message received!

Galit Chait-Moracci, my dear friend and inspiration. Watching you grow have inspired me so much! You are my personal hero! Maybe one day I'll grow up to be like you! Thank you!

Wesley Campbell, for inspiration, courage, strength of heart, and faith. You are a role model, and will change lives of many!

Ana Weber, I am not even sure how you have appeared in my life, but it was a bright day and an absolutely Divine Timing! You have brought me an amazing gift of Light, and really a permission to move on and up! Thank you so much!

Phillip Mills, for your friendship, for believing in me, for encouraging! I am so grateful to know you for so many years!

Sotantar and Pahana, Master Bing John Gillmore and Craig Phillips, my spiritual teachers. I am so grateful for your appearance on my path when I needed you, for opening my eyes, and for giving me the map where to go next, and for opening my eyes to realize the world beyond seen.

Kevin Sverduk, my professor in Sports Psychology, who became a catalyst for the changes to happen in my life...

Laura Dewey and D'Aun Moore, girls, thank you so much for being such an incredible support team! We did it!

Tamara Eristavi, thank you for your gracious time, wisdom, and advice with the book, and in life, and for literally saving my life! I value your friendship so much, Sister!

Marina Mikoultchik, for friendship, for encouragement to begin writing, for always being available to support me.

For my talented photographer **Eric Weiss** (www.ewphoto.info). You truly brought my spirit forward through your loving guidance, intuition, and vision.

For **Marlene Dunstan** for generous contribution of time and story, for your support, and love.

Todd Wickstrom, thank you for your gentle guidance, friendship, encouragement, honesty and wisdom. Your advise and assistance with publishing was invaluable!

For all my students and clients, particularly: **Sasha Cohen, Johnny Weir, Angelyn Nguyen, Deanna Inn-Anderson, Amanda Gelb, Victoria Hecht, Katarina Kulgeyko, Sarah Hsyao, Elizabeth Westerlund, Sahmaro Rockfold, Diandra Catrinescu, Layla Karnes,** and many others. You really were my Teachers. I would have never pushed myself this far, if it wasn't for you. You have inspired me to go further.

For all the classmates and peer coaches in the Soul-Centered Professional Coaching program, especially: **Lori Richards, Rory Cohen, Michael Anderson, Carla Rotering, Tracy Suttles, Deanna Dansky, and Gage Bock**

For all the devoted, disciplined, committed to their children skating parents of my students. Without your support, trust, and belief in me I wouldn't have become a coach and a person I've become. I bow to you in my deepest appreciation.

All my coaches, mentors, judges, officials, US Figure Skating, and Professional Skaters Association, notably: **Pam Duane-Gregory, Ron Ludington, Kerry Leitch, John Nicks, Alexey Mishin, Dawn Eyerly, and LA Figure Skating Club**. You've shaped me into the coach I've become!

<u>**Spirit**, for making all of this be possible for us to experience!!!!</u>

About the Author

Latvian-born Faye Kitariev is a former US figure skating coach and choreographer. Over a twenty-year professional career, Faye coached and choreographed numerous national and international skaters, including US national champion and Olympic silver medalist Sasha Cohen and world bronze medalist Johnny Weir.

After the 2006 Olympic Games, Faye turned her attention to performance psychology, and why some athletes reach their full potential while others fall far short. Her study of personal growth and development led her to fields as diverse as sports psychology, yoga, meditation, tai chi, aikido, and hypnosis, and resulting in her receiving an MA in spiritual psychology from the University of Santa Monica.

Faye owns and operates **Make the Impossible Possible**, a coaching and consulting firm. Her mission is to inspire and empower people to live authentic, successful lives. She lives in Southern California with her daughter.

To contact Faye's office, to join her e-list or for information about other products, coaching, speaking, workshops and seminars visit: fayekitariev.com or choreographyofawakening.com

Made in the USA
San Bernardino, CA
10 May 2014